THE POLICE ACADEMY: AN INSIDE VIEW

THE POLICE ACADEMY: AN INSIDE VIEW
Richard N. Harris

John Wiley & Sons, Inc.
New York London Sydney Toronto

Copyright © 1973, by John Wiley & Sons, Inc.

Library of Congress Cataloging in Publication Data

Harris, Richard N.   1942-
The police academy.

1. Police—Study and teaching—United States.
2. Police training—United States. I. Title.

HV8143.H33   363.2'07   72-8271
ISBN 0-471-35322-1

Printed in the United States of America

10 9 8 7 6 5 4 3 2 1

To Madeline, in whom I have found both reason and emotion

PREFACE*

The idea to study police training first came to me while I was reading *Crimes Without Victims*. There was a passage in which a law enforcement officer claimed that if the laws of victimless crimes were not enforced by the police, the public "would react by lynch law or some other type of punitive activity."[1] This remark caused me to ask several questions. Was the officer implying that the laws of victimless crimes—laws that are generally unenforceable because the "victim" desires a legally proscribed service—should be stricken from the criminal code? For years, legal scholars have argued that these laws are criminal and immoral in themselves.[2] Were police officers now in agreement? Does the strategic position of the police vis-a-vis homosexuality, drug addiction, and abortion acquaint them with the human and material waste that is a direct or indirect consequence of these laws? Do law enforcers have the insight to be aware of the perils of legislating private morality? Are they exposed to the legal and social problems of crimes without victims during their training? If so, is this instruction enlightened or prejudiced? If not, what exactly are they taught? Are police recruits given information that will enable them to support intelligent reforms of laws without necessarily turning toward more repressive measures? Are they effectively taught to respect persons whose ideologies, attitudes, and behavior differ from their own? Indeed, are police recruits exposed to sound "liberal" orientations as well as to "conservative" ones?

When I examined the literature to find some answers to these questions, I was surprised to learn that a large gap in information

* The material in this project was prepared under Grant No. 91-23-69-37 from the Manpower Administration, U.S. Department of Labor under the authority of title I of the Manpower Development and Training Act of 1962 as amended. Researchers who undertake these projects under government sponsorship are encouraged to express freely their professional judgment. Therefore, points of view or opinions stated in this document do not necessarily represent the official position or policy of the Department of Labor.

[1] Edwin M. Schur, *Crimes Without Victims* (Englewood Cliffs, N.J.: Prentice-Hall, 1965), p. 161.

[2] H. L. A. Hart, *Law, Liberty and Morality* (Stanford, Cal.: Stanford University Press, 1963); Lon L. Fuller, *The Morality of Law* (New Haven, Conn.: Yale University Press, 1964); and Edwin M. Schur, *Our Criminal Society* (Englewood Cliffs, N.J.: Prentice-Hall, 1969).

existed regarding police training. Even very insightful studies
of the police included only a chapter on the subject. I then decided
to study training in a police academy for two reasons.

1. An in-depth study of police training not only was needed in
   the sociological literature but it would fill a gap that could have
   important implications for social policy. In a time when a major
   social problem in America is law enforcement, it seemed that an
   impartial study of police training should be made available to
   politicians and police officials.

2. The police occupation is, supposedly, molding a "new breed
   of cop." If this is true, the logical point to study ideological
   changes within the organization is when in-coming members are
   trained.

At the outset, I must emphasize several points.

At times the focus of this book may appear confusing: Is it the
process of recruit training, or is it the setting of training as a source
of information about the role of police? Actually, it is impossible to
separate the recruit from the patrolman, since it is for the role
of patrolman that a recruit is trained. Therefore, in my discussion
of academy training, the reference point also includes the needs of
the patrolman as the recruits and their instructors define them. Since
most of the instructors were taken from the field for specific lectures,
it is safe to assume that they reflect the conceptions held by the
typical man in the field—they may merely articulate them better.
Also, if there is a particular focus to this book, it is the understanding
of the recruits, their instructors, and police work as conveyed
within the academy.

If I should appear to gloss over the more obvious points, this is
intentional. One of the purposes of sociological analysis is to search
for the unrecognized or unintended factors of social life rather than
to reiterate what is already known. For instance: Is the emphasis
by the academy on the recruit's physical appearance a manifestation
of discipline or a means by which he is made aware of the
importance of dressing neatly? My data suggest that it has still
another, unrecognized, function which I found necessary to
emphasize: physical appearance is linked to the recruit's moral
framework for judging others and himself.

I apologize for any unintended consequences of my study. I did
not enter the academy to whitewash or blackwash anybody or
anything. I believe that any researcher who does a sincere study
of the police cannot help but appreciate the difficulties that they face,
and I have tried to discuss these difficulties and the police responses

to them fairly. I hope that the criticisms in this book are viewed as constructive by police buffs and critics alike. I feel fortunate, indeed, to have been permitted to do a participatory study.

I thank the many people whose help made this study possible, for it is as much theirs as it is mine.

I specifically express my gratitude to the following members of "Rurban County" Police Department whose trust and willingness to risk criticism enabled an "intellectual" to learn about police work through firsthand experience: Stanley Andrysik, Joseph Avella, John L. Barry, Harold DesVerney, John Fakler, William Gardiner, John J. Mulhern, Warren McCue, and the thirty-second recruit class.

I also thank the following persons for their insights, persistence, and support: Jack Burton, Mary Jane Cramer, Peter K. Manning, Peter Kong-ming New and, especially, Edwin M. Schur.

Doubtless, in every research project, there is an individual who offers very special help. In this instance, I extend my thanks to Natalie Allon, who helped to formulate many ideas in this book and provided a rich source of moral support.

RICHARD N. HARRIS

CONTENTS

THE POLICE ACADEMY: AN INSIDE VIEW

"Gentlemen, let me remind you,
the police are not here to create disorder:
they are here to preserve disorder."
Mayor Richard Daley,
defending police actions at Chicago
during the 1968 Democratic National Convention

Police and the Moral Division of Labor.

CHAPTER ONE

Every occupation appears to have what Everett C. Hughes terms a "moral division of labor." That is, some members of an occupation are able to conform to norms of respectability because other members fulfill the requirements of the less respectable, or "dirty," facets.[1] For instance, Jerome Carlin notes that "respectable" lawyers do not usually handle divorces, which can become rather messy, since there are always less well-off lawyers who snatch up those kinds of cases. Because these lawyers are less well-off financially, they feel fewer compunctions in some of their unscrupulous practices.[2] In other words, the respectable lawyer has clean hands at the expense of someone else's dirty hands.

The phenomenon Hughes observes within occupations also operates on a more macrosocial level. Society is able to function with smoothness and a sense of moral cleanliness because there are *entire* occupations, insulated from public observability, that wash the dirty linen or keep it out of sight. The respectable people of society recognize the need for distasteful work to be done. This work may involve objects (picking up garbage) or people (processing rejected or dead persons). While the respectables want the job done, they are less concerned with the particulars of how it is to be accomplished. Indeed, in the respectables' desire for cleanliness—physical, psychological, and social—they prefer to know as little as possible about the job.

---

[1] Everett Cherrington Hughes, *Men and Their Work* (Chicago: The Free Press, 1958), pp. 44–45, 49–51, 71–73, 92–95, 121–122, 137.

[2] Jerome E. Carlin, *Lawyers' Ethics* (New York: The Russell Sage Foundation, 1966), p. 177.

Discretion is the better part of valor: "Don't tell us your problems, just do what you're paid to do; we don't care how you do it, but do it!"

Germany had its "Jewish problem," and its people wanted something done about it. Once the solution became public, the respectables reacted with shock, disbelief, shame, and protestations of personal innocence—although throughout World War II, they were aware that their Jewish neighbors mysteriously, yet conveniently, had left their homes, businesses, and bank accounts.[3] Likewise, many American respectables reacted with shame and indignation when dogs were released on peaceful civil disobedients in Selma, Alabama, in order to solve its "Negro problem."

Notwithstanding Mayor Daley's slip of the tongue when he defended what the *Walker Report* called a police riot,[4] perhaps the real offense of the 1968 Democratic National Convention was not in the blatant violence by which the police suppressed the student demonstrators, nor in the duplicity and chicanery on the convention floor to ensure the defeat of an antiwar candidate's nomination. Violence and chicanery had all happened before, and they could be expected to happen again. The real offense of the convention was that these events were shown on all three national television circuits to be witnessed by anyone who cared to watch. The conditions of low observability of dirty work had been violated.

Police work seems to be an example of dirty work. The low prestige of police work stems partly from the "dirty" facet of policing: enforcing laws that support interest groups, but becoming scapegoats when things go wrong. That is, the respectables hire the police to do their dirty work for them. Although respectables ask the police to enforce the laws, they become indignant when they are asked to obey them. Vaguely aware that police officers have the tasks of touching diseased bodies, crawling under trains to tie up a bloody stump on the end of a leg, and subjecting themselves to continual time shifts in tours of duty which take their toll on the body later in life, respectables do not want to be reminded of such troubles. In dealing with police problems, respectables would dirty their own hands by being reminded of the sordid aspects of life that the police officer must contend with each

[3] Everett C. Hughes, "Good People and Dirty Work," *The Other Side*, edited by Howard S. Becker (New York: The Free Press of Glencoe, 1964), pp. 23–36.

[4] Rights in Conflict: The Violent Confrontation of Demonstrators and Police in the Parks and Streets of Chicago during the Week of the Democratic National Convention, *Walker Report* (New York: Bantam Books, Inc., 1968).

day. Although they are aware of the need for law and order, they refuse to take responsibility for their personal involvement: they do not train their children to respect the police; they keep information from the police; and they do not participate in police-community relations programs.

If this is the respectables' perspective of the police, one may well ask what the public really means when it demands law and order. The recent saliency of the law and order issue in political campaigning may reflect several areas of confusion for respectable middle-class America. It may reflect the increasing crime rates and disrespect for authority on all levels. It may be a reaction to middle-class youth's rejection of the value orientations of their parents. It may be a reaction to the national guilt rooted in the ambivalence toward the Vietnam War. It may also reflect the anger over the apparent welfare subsidation of the very people who riot. And surely, it reflects consternation over some recent Supreme Court decisions that, many claim, seem more protective of the rights of the criminal than of the rights of the victim.

On a more latent and unrecognized level, the present demand for law and order appears to invoke repression and prejudice, as a substitute for effective programs of action, in order to deal with major social problems. At times, the police are used to support the interests of power groups. For example, at the turn of the century, police were used by management to break up union activities.[5] Presently, the law has been used to suppress those who do not subscribe to political orthodoxy, and it has become clear to lessees that the law favors landlords. The cry for law and order is used to cover up important social issues just as the expense for "national defense" provides some politicians with the excuse that funds are not available to solve urban, poverty, and medical problems. The question then becomes: To what extent is law enforcement "dirty"? That is, to what extent is law enforcement following the public's unspoken and secret wishes?

The dirty facet of police work does not only refer to actually *doing* the dirty work of the respectables. To ask a police officer to resolve the "student problem" is only part of the process of "dirtying" the officer's occupation. There is another side of the coin. Dirty work may also be physically disgusting, such as dragging a vomiting drunk to a

---

[5] A Task Force Report Submitted to the National Commission on the Causes and Prevention of Violence, *The Politics of Protest*, under the direction of Jerome H. Skolnick (New York: Simon and Schuster, 1969), pp. 268–269.

call box, or morally disgusting, such as handling and being exposed to family squabbles. Police work may be dirty by other respectable standards, too, because it often requires physical and even violent means of control. What the police officer must face every day seems to be too demanding, too sordid, and too dangerous for the citizen to involve himself in law, order, and justice.

Given this state of affairs, how are policemen trained to work within this social context and what are their modes of adjustment? Researchers have not considered these questions sufficiently. A partial explanation for this neglect is that policemen themselves regard academy training as discontinuous with everyday occupational demands. Apparently students of police work accept the notion that the police academy is isolated from the ordinary policeman's world of work. Speaking about a Midwestern police department of the late 1940's, William Westley reports:

> ... everyone expects [the recruit] to take himself seriously
> at first, but he will not obtain the trust and confidence of the
> other men until he begins to see the formal rules as they are. . . .[6]

And, in 1967, Arthur Niederhoffer speaks of the highly rated New York City Police Department:

> The more experienced men tell [the recruit] that in order to
> become a real policeman, he will have to forget everything he is
> learning at the Academy ... that attendance at the recruit school
> is "just a waste of time. . . ."[7]

If academy training is an experiential stage of the police career, surely the time and energy spent in the academy has some subjective meaning to the recruit, for better or worse. The impact of academy training on the recruit cannot be so easily dismissed as inconsequential unless evidence exists to support this position. Thus far, no study has been available to offer evidence one way or the other.

Why, then, is academy training considered to be ineffective and discrepant with the everyday demands of police work? Kai Erikson suggests that social control agencies are oriented toward regulating social deviance rather than toward its elimination. He goes on to say

---

[6] William A. Westley, *Violence and the Police* (Cambridge, Mass.: The MIT Press, 1970), p. 156.
[7] Arthur Niederhoffer, *Behind the Shield* (Garden City, N.Y.: Doubleday, 1967), pp. 44 and 47.

that social deviants may be useful to society by their testing and retesting of the degree of flexibility of rules and laws, or even because they point to needed changes in some of those rules and laws. He asks whether society possibly organizes itself in such a way as to *promote* deviancy:

> Indeed, the institutions devised by society for discouraging
> deviant behavior are often so poorly equipped for the task that
> we might well ask why this is considered their "real" function
> at all.[8]

If institutions of social control have the unintended or unrecognized function of merely regulating deviance, inadequate police training may be perceived as part of the "poor equipment" for one of the institutions of social control—law enforcement. Perhaps this is why police officials, politicians, and the citizenry seem to place little interest in police training; they do not want policemen to perform *too* well. Indeed, as I demonstrate in the following pages, even up-graded police training is likely to boomerang and maintain both the low prestige and the "dirty" qualities of police work.

The major purposes of this study are: to understand the training process in one police academy at one point in time and, based on this case study, to suggest possible measures for reform. From the pages that follow, I hope the reader will gain an appreciation for: (1) what it is like to go through a police training program, (2) what kinds of material are presented to the recruit, (3) how the recruit responds to his training, (4) what image the recruit has of himself, his fellow police officers, and police work as a partial result of his training, and (5) the possibly unrecognized or unintended consequences of this training that operate on the recruit while he is in the academy and then in the field. Before I offer a description and analysis of police training, however, I shall sketch briefly the police department, the academy, the academy personnel, the recruits, and my research strategy.

---

[8] Kai Erikson, "Notes on the Sociology of Deviance," in Howard S. Becker's *The Other Side*, p. 15.

Just as the process of communicating information
itself expresses information, so also a corpus
of communicated signs has expressive
aspects. Discursive statements seem inevitably to
manifest a style of some kind, and can
never apparently be entirely free of "egocentric
particulars" and other context tied meanings.
Irving Goffman, Strategic Interaction

The Setting.

CHAPTER TWO

The police department that granted me permission to carry out my participatory research of academy training shall be referred to as Rurban County Police Department, or RCPD. This chapter examines background data of the county, the academy, the staff, the academy way of life, and the methodology. A recruit profile is also included.

THE COUNTY

Rurban County is one of the fastest growing counties in the nation. It is comprised mostly of residential areas and farmlands but also has small industry and a few aircraft plants. Its area is about 900 square miles, and it lies about 35 miles from Megopolis City. Although Rurban County is not nearly as urbanized as its neighbor, Suburban County, it is experiencing law enforcing problems applicable to its more urban neighbors—hence the pseudonym, Rurban County. About 5.3 percent of its population is black or colored, and they tend to be localized in a few communities. Nevertheless, in the latter half of the 1960's there were two "race riots." In addition, the police have been called on during college, university, and high school demonstrations.

RCPD patrols the western half of the county only. The eastern end of the county maintains its many local police departments, but it has the use of the RCPD Detective Bureau, Bureau of Communications and Information, Bureau of Identification, and Bureau of Police Training, which includes the academy. Because of its rural character and expansiveness in the western half covered by RCPD, the prime means of patrol is by car. No car is left unused, even if it means taking a

9

foot patrolman from his post. In 1968, at least 59 percent of all departmental complaints were noncriminal. In January 1960, when RCPD was first established, there were 619 sworn members. By September 1968 there were 1676 sworn members, 240 civilian employees, and 510 school crossing guards.[1]

THE POLICE ACADEMY

In 1959 the state passed a Municipal Police Training Council Act, which mandated all police departments within it to establish a minimum standard of recruit training by 1960. This act was the first of its kind in the nation. Since then, 38 states have followed with similar legislation. The act required a minimum of 80 hours of training. Three years later the minimum was expanded to 120 hours. A few years later the requirement was increased to its present level of 210 classroom hours and 30 hours in the field. The Rurban County Police Academy started with the 80 hours' minimum of 1960, but far exceeds it now with 440 classroom hours and 40 hours in the field.[2]

THE ACADEMY STAFF

Before I discuss the academy staff, I must give special recognition to the police commissioner, since without his approval and support this in-depth study of police recruit training probably could not have been written. He was the only police commissioner I contacted who promised to allow me to be exposed to police training and who fulfilled his promise.

Commissioner Flynn[3] enjoys a remarkable popularity within the

---

[1] *Annual Report* 1968, a publication of RCPD.
[2] Seymour Martin Lipset refers to a survey by Norman Kassoff of the research staff of the International Association of Chiefs of Police, which gathered the minimum training hours for various occupations and compared them with police training hours: physicians, 11,000; barbers, 4000; beauticians, 1200; police, less than 200 hours, the majority having less than five weeks of training. "Why Cops Hate Liberals—and Vice Versa," *Atlantic Monthly*, 223 (March 1969), pp. 76–83.
[3] All names are fictitious.

department. During my three months of formal research and several months of follow-up work, I never heard one derogatory remark against him. His men, on all levels of rank, hold him in high esteem for his dedication, hard work, and sincerity. It was rumored that he was appointed police commissioner because he was the only honest county administrator around.

His attitude at our graduation ceremony provides some insight into his character and popularity. Before the ceremony was formally started, he chided the mothers and wives of the recruits who were trying to keep their youngsters and babies quiet. He said that the police department included the families of its officers, and it was natural for a child to be excited. If a child cried, "There's Daddy!" it would be quite appropriate, for the family was a part of the police force. He liked it when children cried out; therefore, the mothers and wives should not be concerned about their children's behavior—the graduation ceremony was for the recruits and their families.

The original academy staff of 1960 was comprised of one captain, two lieutenants, and a patrolman. At the time of my research (February-April 1969), the staff consisted of an inspector, a captain, a lieutenant—although there were supposed to be two—two sergeants, and four patrolmen. However, of those nine staff members, a sergeant and two patrolmen manned the pistol range. Although the three men were officially defined as part of the training staff, the recruits did not seem to consider them within the staff category.

Since both the inspector and his executive officer, Captain Anderson, were in administrative positions, they had little direct contact with the recruits. However, they both gave me a great deal of support and encouragement throughout my study. It was with the advice and consent of Inspector Garrity that Commissioner Flynn was encouraged to permit a participant observation study of recruit training.

Unfortunately, Lieutenant Noonan had little contact with the recruit class also. The full year of accumulated leave time by the other lieutenant caught the academy unprepared and burdened his co-lieutenant with responsibility for both the in-service training of patrolmen and officers and the recruit training program. His in-service training responsibilities dominated most of his time. Lieutenant Noonan had attempted to obtain a transfer to the academy for quite a while before his appointment, and it was only when his main opponent died that he found the doors open to him. It was truly unfortunate that the transfer was delayed, for with only a brief two-hour lecture on the second day of the session, he left an impact on the recruits that lasted throughout the three months. Thereafter, whenever he appeared before the recruits, the whole character and tempo of the setting changed to one of liveliness and pride.

Lieutenant Noonan had become a legend to those who knew him in the field. By chance, my precinct assignment during our one-week field training had been his main precinct in past years, and stories abounded about him. He was considered a "real cop's cop" who knew how to get the job done most efficiently with the least offense to others. Yet, he felt no compunction about embarrassing his commanding officers regarding their own incompetence. One story concerned a precinct commander who was very politically sensitive and refused to issue orders that might upset the status quo. Once the commander walked into his office in time to overhear a (staged) telephone conversation, ". . . I don't care who you are; you know what you can do with your damn political party," and the receiver was slammed down. That attitude, with a keen sense of dedication, and imagination intermingled with an ever present wit, won him the admiration of the recruits and his fellow officers. Said one of the academy staff appreciatively, "When he's not around, the rest of us have to work that much harder." His hyperactivity through acute devotion toward professionalizing law enforcement has caused his colleagues at the academy some concern (and justly so) for his health.

The other three members of the staff, a sergeant and two patrolmen, had more direct and continual involvement with the recruits. Indeed, they shouldered most of the recruit program themselves. One of the patrolmen, Joe Puccio, taught physical training, self-defense, karate, koga (a technique for using a nightstick), "come-along" holds which force an unwilling prisoner to accompany the officer, and riot stick use.

Patrolman Arsenault was a retired army master sergeant with some drill instructing experience. He taught military drill, riot formations, the history and causes of civil disturbances, and the "exciting" subjects of departmental rules and regulations and the filling out of departmental forms. Instead of the harassing or badgering that I expected of an army drill instructor, his emphasis was on instructing and correcting. He was a good teacher and guide, and he was sensitive to the present social problems plaguing the nation.

Finally, there was Sergeant Sheehan, who appeared to be the individual most responsible for recruit training. Sergeant Sheehan joined RCPD in 1962. Sometime later he was appointed to the tactical force, a trouble-shooting elite. Along with protecting dignitaries such as President Kennedy, it participated in special investigations and undercover work, sensitive community relations problems, and investigations of prospective candidates to the police force. In the latter capacity, Sergeant Sheehan gained a reputation for concern about police professionalism. Often, he would check up on those candidates whom he had interviewed and recommended to the department. After the tactical force was disbanded, he was transferred to Inspection, which had the responsibility for seeing that departmental regulations and standards were maintained. This assignment involved investigatory skills, since Inspection followed up on citizen complaints of police behavior. He remained with the Inspection Squad until he was promoted to sergeant. While going through an in-service training program, he was tapped by the academy command for a permanent assignment as an instructor for recruits.

Sergeant Sheehan's sensitivity to interpersonal dynamics surprised me. He often showed insight into my role with the other recruits, and he was helpful in my maintaining a proper research perspective. He also demonstrated a capacity and concern for self- and departmental introspection. For these reasons, I asked him to read and comment on my first draft. Without his help, and the help of the recruit class president who also read the entire first draft, some of the material would have been misleading.

The dedication that Sergeant Sheehan had toward law enforcement was evidenced by his many hours of overwork. In spite of his heavy time pressure, he always met with me if I had to see him personally. During our graduation ceremony, he and another patrolman were awarded meritorious service bars by the commissioner for writing, on their own time, an imaginative and informative booklet on a police career in Rurban County for distribution to high school students. Furthermore, both he and Lieutenant Noonan met with high school students once a week for discussions on police work.

Although Niederhoffer suggests that academy personnel in New York City are those who want to avoid the heartaches of patrol work or who are too idealistic for field work, that does not seem to be the case in Rurban County.[4] The teaching personnel are of excellent caliber with solid acumen demonstrated in the field, yet they represent and are concerned about the new professional image of the law enforcer. When I returned to the academy a little over a month after my formal research, the executive officer, Captain Anderson, had been promoted to precinct commander and transferred, and one of

---

[4] Arthur Niederhoffer, *Behind the Shield* (Garden City, N.Y.: Doubleday, 1967), pp. 45–48.

the two patrolmen had been promoted to detective. Thus, in RCPD the police academy is staffed by dedicated, hard-working, experienced, and insightful men "in the know" and "street wise," but with a capacity and desire to perform their work with an eye toward "professionalism" in police work.

RECRUIT PROFILE

There were 53 recruits in the thirty-second recruit class of RCPD. Eleven were from associated agencies. This latter category was used for all recruits who were not members of RCPD. Recruits from associated agencies included the men who came from local police departments in the western portion of Rurban County, all recruits from the local police departments that made up the eastern part of the county, and two recruits from the state university police. After the 12-week training period was completed, I was permitted to go through the precandidate investigations and interviews of the 42 Rurban County recruits. The following profile is based on these investigations and interviews.

The average age of the recruits applying to the academy was 25 years. Thirty-five of the recruits were married at the time of the investigations (about a year before their appointment to the department), and several married during or soon after the training session. The average age when they married was just under 22 years. They generally married four years after high school and three years before applying to RCPD. Of the married recruits, 24 (57 percent) had children; 15 of them had more than one child.

Their fathers' occupations are interesting. Most studies of policemen point out their blue-collar origins.[5] I think the data here may

---

[5] Arthur Niederhoffer, p. 148; John H. McNamara, "Uncertainties of Police Work: Recruits' Backgrounds and Training," *The Police*, edited by David J. Bordua, esp. pp. 166–168 and 191–195; Jerome H. Skolnick, *Justice Without Trial* (New York: John Wiley, 1966); James Q. Wilson, *Varieties of Police Behavior* (Cambridge, Mass.: Harvard University Press, 1968); and Seymour Martin Lipset, "Why Cops Hate Liberals—and Vice Versa," *Atlantic Monthly*, 223 (March 1969), pp. 76–83. The one exception was in Jack J. Preiss and Howard J. Ehrlich's *An Examination of Role Theory: The Case of the State Police* (Lincoln: The University of Nebraska Press, 1966), pp. 11–17, who found that the fathers of 46 percent of their sample were white-collar workers while 54 percent were blue-collar workers.

provide a rationale for revising blue-collar/white-collar dichotomies. The mode of fathers' occupations is indeed manual labor (17), but if we combine blue-collar and white-collar supervisory positions (11) and white-collar nonsupervisory positions (4), the sum would almost equal the 17 fathers in nonsupervisory blue-collar positions. Consequently, the distinction between supervisory and nonsupervisory jobs may be more sociologically meaningful than the white-collar/blue-collar dichotomy when studying worker attitudes and behavior.

At any rate, police recruit fathers are not merely blue collar; they are also supervisors. The brothers of the recruits show a similar phenomenon. Excluding the brothers still in school or college (9) are in the military (12), they are equally divided between those in blue-collar nonsupervisory jobs (12) and those in white-collar or supervisory positions (12). Sixteen (39 percent) of the recruits' mothers are reported as working.

The educational and employment records of the recruits are also enlightening. While 29 (69 percent) of the recruits were Roman Catholic, only 12 attended a Catholic school, averaging six years per student, and only one spent some time in a Catholic high school. Three recruits were high school dropouts, but because of civil service requirements, they received equivalency diplomas before being appointed to the academy. The median and mean overall high school grade was 72.5 with 82 the highest grade average. Five recruits were in the top half of their graduating classes, and one was in the top quarter of his class.

Excluding military time, the recruits averaged 3.2 jobs per person before appointment. However, the minimum age requirement for the department was 21 years; consequently, the recruits had to fill in the time between high school and appointment with other jobs. Ten experienced substantial periods of unemployment, although sometimes as a result of layoffs during slack work periods. The average span of time per job was 2½ years. Twelve recruits had had some previous policing experience, averaging almost 2 years per man.

Before appointment to RCPD, 12 recruits were unable to save money from their salaries. Since the recruits received full patrolman's salary during their training period ($580 per month), 37 (88 percent) recruits increased their monthly earnings an average of $150 per month. For the five recruits who took salary cuts in order to join RCPD, monthly loss averaged $63.

Three items were of special interest to me. First, only one recruit in the class belonged to a social club, the Elks, although three others were volunteer firemen.[6] Second, the department (wisely, I believe) was not rigid about excluding candidates who had minor police records. Twelve (29 percent) recruits had records of questioning, arrests, or convictions by juvenile authorities. By contrast, Niederhoffer reports that the only way candidates for the New York City Police may enter if they have minor records is the "one in three" rule. Under this rule the commissioner has the obligation to choose at least one of each three consecutive names on the Civil Service list.[7]

Finally, excluding the responses of the recruits who came from other law enforcement agencies before joining RCPD (12 out of 57 reasons),[8] 21 (47 percent) of the responses offered security as the main reason for joining. The other reasons included childhood ambition (7), advancement opportunities in a growing department (6), altruism (4), the salary (4), and interesting work (3). Of the 12 experienced recruits, the reasons for joining included childhood ambitions (4), commuting problems to Megopolis City (4), security (2), and advancement opportunities (2). Based on these figures, it appears that at least two-thirds of the recruits join law enforcement agencies for materialistic or extrinsic considerations, although a substantial minority do so for idealistic reasons.[9]

Something that was not in the investigation reports but that I found to be a principal reason for joining was the police retirement program. For someone with a limited educational background, who was unhappy with his previous jobs, RCPD offered not only financial and employment security but also an attractive retirement policy. Again and again I heard recruits say that they were looking forward to

---

[6] When I mentioned this point to a group of RCPD patrolmen as an indication of police isolation from values conflicting to their own, they hostilely rejoined: that's not fair, they are just starting out in life; all you studied was recruits, not patrolmen; many of us go to college—how much contact do you want?

[7] Arthur Niederhoffer, pp. 148–149.

[8] Some of the 42 recruits offered more than one reason.

[9] Compare this association between idealism and cynicism with James H. Bryan, "Apprenticeship in Prostitution," *Social Problems*, 12 (Winter 1965), pp. 287–297; Howard S. Becker et al., *Boys in White* (Chicago, Ill.: University of Chicago Press, 1961), pp. 420–430; Arthur Niederhoffer, p. 44; and Ned Polsky, *Hustlers, Beats and Others* (Garden City, N.Y.: Doubleday, 1969), p. 82. Other researchers have also noted the motivation for security among police officers. Some of them include: Arthur Niederhoffer, William Westley, *Violence and the Police* (Cambridge, Mass.: MIT Press, 1970; and James Q. Wilson, "Generational and Ethnic Differences among Career Police Officers," *American Journal of Sociology*, 69 (March 1964), pp. 522–528.

retiring at half pay in only 20 years.[10] As one recruit said to me, police work "was the best place if you don't have a college degree."

RECRUIT REQUIREMENTS

Before a person can join RCPD, he must take a competitive civil service examination. The higher his score, the more likely that he will be able to enter the recruit class before the quota is met. In addition to the examination, the applicant must successfully pass physical endurance tests, a medical examination, and an in-depth investigation into his background. Part of the investigation includes a preliminary interview with the applicant and his wife at their home; this is followed by another interview at the academy. Only then can he be accepted as a candidate. Following the successful completion of 12 weeks in the academy, he is on probation for nine more months, during which time he can easily be dismissed from the department.

To graduate from the academy, he must meet four basic requirements. He must have a good attendance record. He must score 200 out of 300 points on the pistol combat course and 70 out of 100 points on the bull's-eye range, both under time pressure. He must have a typed notebook that is transcribed from class notes. Finally, he must attain an overall average of 75 points on his three monthly written examinations based on class lectures.

The subjects to which the recruit class was exposed can be categorized as follows. Next to each category and its examples are the number of hours devoted to each grouping. The number of hours are not altogether accurate, but they do demonstrate the emphasis given to these various topics.

---

[10] The whole question of retirement as an important motivation for joining an occupation is an intriguing area for study. I recall a seminary student constantly talking about making plans for his retirement, for instance. For someone to work at a job for 20 years in order to retire at an early age and to receive a pension seems rather depressing to me. Perhaps occupations that attract people for this reason, be they dirty workers or clean workers, can be studied with an eye toward the members' psychological dimensions. As Peter K. New inquired, "I wonder what the man in the tollbooth is thinking about all day."

Topic	Hours
Patrol procedures (including 40 hours in the field)	89
Law and the courts (excluding laws related to traffic)	78½
Traffic (laws, accident forms, driving skills, procedures)	40½
Police subdepartments: structure and functions (homicide, narcotics, canine, juvenile aid, arson, inspection, communications, etc.)	32½
Self-defense (karate, koga, riot training)	26
Drill and inspections	21
Departmental forms and regulations	20
First aid (including maternity cases)	16
Orientation (community relations, police ethics, professionalism, race relations, county geography)	16

THE DAILY SCHEDULE

Although the recruits were required to be in formation by 8:45 A.M., about half of them arrived a good half hour early. They drank coffee and sat or stood around in small groups along the drill floor. Shortly before 8:45 the two platoon sergeants called their respective platoons to formation. Each platoon consisted of three rows of about nine men in each row. The first man of the row was its squad leader. His main responsibility was to check the attendance within his squad. Through a series of salutes and reports, each squad leader passed his information to the platoon sergeant. As Patrolman Arsenault came to take his position in front of the platoons at precisely 8:45, the sergeants called their platoons to attention. Patrolman Arsenault ordered each sergeant to report the state of the platoon's attendance. If anyone was reported absent, his name was taken and a patrol car was dispatched to his home to check on his safety. This precaution is a department regulation because of the inherent dangers of police work. Even if absentees live outside the police district, other police departments cooperate in this procedure.

Roll call was followed by inspection or drill, which lasted anywhere from 5 to 20 minutes. If inspection was brief, there might still be time for a few drill movements. If not, the platoons were called to attention and dismissed for a brief break before classes.

The first of the three morning classes began around 9:00. For every 50 minutes of class time, the recruits were given a ten-minute coffee break. It was not long before they tried to extend their breaks to 15 minutes or more. After the first week of classes, for instance, the instructors always had to call the recruits back to the class. Once in the room the recruits talked to one another from their seats until the instructor or staff member walked in. The recruit who sat closest to the door yelled "Atten-hut!" at which time the rest of the recruits jumped to attention. After they were reseated, the lecture began.

The lunch period was from 12:00 to 12:45. Some recruits brought their own lunches; others bought hero sandwiches provided at the academy. Some recruits who rebelled at the prices of the sandwiches drove to a nearby store and brought back food to eat. Every now and then a recruit who lived near enough to the academy went home for lunch.

At precisely 12:45 roll call was taken again. Following roll call, the recruits either practiced drill or riot formations, or they were dismissed for their 1:00 class. There were four hours of classes in the afternoon. The last hour or two was often spent in participatory activities such as koga, self-defense, and riot tactics. For physical training, karate, and self-defense, the recruits changed into sweat clothes in the men's room before classes. Although military drill sometimes took place outside the building during cold days, riot formations were practiced outside only when the weather warmed. At 4:50 or whenever the last class of the day was dismissed, the recruits rushed out of the building. Inside of 10 minutes, there was hardly a car left in the parking area.

Until the first test was given at the end of the first month, the mood of the recruits seemed anxious. Although the tests were based on lecture material alone, instructors passed out large mimeographed sheets and constantly referred to portions of the penal code. Not only did the recruits have to worry about their lessons but they were expected to do physical exercises, practice koga and karate moves, keep their leather spit-shined, and practice dry-firing with their revolvers (to develop finger control)—all on their own time. If the first month of recruit training could be characterized by anything, it seemed to be a feeling of too little time to learn too many things. As one recruit told me, "I can tell you . . . . They're worried about what they are going to do if they flunk out, with their wife and kids."

The mood of the recruits seemed to shift significantly during the last month of the session. Throughout the training program the staff had tried to counter the prejudices against classroom training by having police officers from the field lecture on most of the subjects. But once the recruits spent their week in the field, complaints about the irrelevancy of the academy increased.

With the approach of graduation day, the recruits became more and more restless. Each day was characterized by boredom. The sense of boredom was aggravated by circumstances other than just the anticipation of graduation. For one reason or another, the staff was unable to keep to the schedule, usually because lecturers did not arrive on time. Breaks between classes lengthened into 30 minutes; and some of the classes were objectively more boring than they had been in previous weeks. Indeed, one entire morning, sponsored by Green Cross, on traffic safety seemed to be geared for elementary school children. In spite of the increasing restlessness and ennui, however, there was a visible sigh of relief after the final written examination as if nothing else could stand between them and graduation.

RESEARCH STRATEGY

The research strategy or method an investigator selects to collect and analyze his information is intricately related to his findings and conclusions. Hence, a description of my methodology is in order.

I chose the technique of participant observation as my main strategy to study the police academy for several reasons. First, I believe that an understanding of people's behavior and attitudes is best attained by sharing their experiences. Too often sociologists have sacrificed the pulse of the people they were studying by the techniques of other research strategies. With my concern for understanding social behavior rather than for making precise predictions, I needed a research strategy capable of capturing the subtle mosaic of life-styles.

Second, the technique of participant observation made information available to me that would have been difficult or impossible to obtain through other stratagems. I believed that rapport and acceptance, especially in a reputedly suspicious environment of outsiders, could be accomplished by demonstrating my willingness to share the rigors of the police training and by remaining completely aboveboard in my intentions with the recruits. Participant observation appeared to be the only strategy available to me to meet these needs of research.

Finally, participant observation seemed to be the method fairest to the subjects themselves. If I used survey methods such as questionnaires and interviews, I would be imposing my framework of thinking on the recruits. I did not feel knowledgeable enough to claim that I knew the relevant questions to ask. Also, I did not wish to begin my research with a sociological theory in mind to prove or to disprove, since the result could be "fitting the data to the theory." If I were to be honest with myself and with the recruits, I had to go into the field open-minded, collect as much data as I could, and *then* see what the data seemed to suggest. By following this procedure, I at least would give my subjects the benefit of the doubt. Their discussions would tell *me* what the important questions were. I would accept the recruits on their own level, without imposing my values on them.

Of course, as in any other method, there are significant disadvantages to participatory research strategies. The first disadvantage is the unintentional and unwitting impact of the observer on the action he observes. First, the mere fact that another person is added to the group may change patterns of behavior. Secondly, no one enters a field tabula rasa. The danger of the researcher's projecting his values on those whom he studies is ever-present. Sometimes the researcher may wish to change the field he is observing because he has become overly identified with his subjects. I myself went so far as to ask the staff for an opportunity to present the radical-liberal positions on controversial issues: they offered me an entire morning. There is also the problem of the researcher's identifying with his subjects to such a degree that he loses his capacity to critically evaluate them.

Even if my mistakes were ignored, it was impossible for me to blend into the group completely. For example, I could not hide my profuse writing during lectures even when there was "nothing important" being said at the time. When I explained to one of the men sitting next to me that I was doing research on police training, he remarked, "I thought there was something. You seem to be writing so much."

A rather amusing incident demonstrates my inability to disguise myself as a bona fide recruit. During a break, we were suddenly ordered to fall into formation. Two detectives went quickly down the ranks pulling out a recruit every now and then. When the detectives reached my end of the line, one of them stopped, stared, and then pointed at me. Meanwhile, Sergeant Sheehan, noticing what was happening, rushed up to the detective. The detective turned around and he went to the four recruits taken from ranks. When we were dismissed, a recruit came up to me smiling, "Hey, Harris, how come you didn't get chosen? You look like a college student." I laughed, "I was, but Sergeant Sheehan came running over to stop me!" Here was an example of a stranger's selecting me along with four other recruits for undercover work that required someone who did not "look like a cop."

In spite of all the subtle ways in which a researcher may alter the field that he is studying, to a large degree I was able to neutralize some of these problems until my morning discussion in class toward the end of the training session. At least three-quarters of the training took place in a lecture style classroom situation. Because it was expected that the recruits would be writing in their notebooks, I was able to write everything mentioned in the classroom almost verbatim without recruits or instructors becoming threatened. The only cause for wonder by the instructors occurred when they noticed a lone recruit scribbling away and felt called on to repeat their statement that, at this time, no notes were required. It took the recruits only a few days to become accustomed to my constant writing, which was helped by sitting in the last row, even when the lectures seemed boring.

Lessons in which the recruits actively had to participate and the informal discussions before roll call and during coffee breaks and lunch were more problematic. In these contexts, I was forced to rely on memory or the surreptitious marking of key words and phrases on an always available scrap paper. Fortunately, I was able to type up these sketchy notes more fully within an hour after each day's activities. Consequently, distortions were kept to a minimum. Furthermore, a staff member and the recruit class president read my first draft in its entirety. The recruit suggested that no change be made, and the staff member suggested that I elaborate or balance some of the data to avoid the reader's being misled.

The second major disadvantage of participant observation is the biased viewpoint of the researcher. The researcher enters the field with his own values and attitudes, but because he must assume a definite role, he is limited to the knowledge available from this perspective. I chose the role of the recruit thereby cutting myself off from the administrative and staff perspectives. However, this limitation was not particularly problematic for me because all I wanted was the perspective of the recruit anyway.

It was striking how I became cognizant of this strategic limitation, however. While on patrol, during our full week of field experience about midway through the session, I was discussing my experiences with some curious footmen. I remarked that I thought the staff devoted too much time to drill and a "patent leather" appearance. The patrolmen agreed. A few minutes later one of them asked, "Do you have hour inspections?" "No, maybe a half-hour or less every other day now." He answered, "We used to get hour inspections every day." I let this item pass without further comment, but I realized that I had thought something was overly stressed, while from the standpoint of the staff, their demands were quite liberal.

Also, by forming alliances with one group of subjects, a researcher closes channels of information with other groups. Fortunately, I was able to establish and maintain rapport with all the recruits with the exception of five members, four of whom were "loners." Of the five, I was eventually able to break down the resistance of three of them. The other 48 recruits permitted me to join and leave their groups at will with no apparent effect; they seemed receptive toward me in individual conversations also, at least after the first week.

Another major criticism of participatory research lies in its procedures, since it is a very individualized experience. Procedures are therefore not standardized nor open to inspection by fellow researchers. Readers must take the participant researcher's word that a solid foundation of fact underlies his report. Thus it is difficult to establish the reliability and validity of the conclusions to the satisfaction of other researchers. For example, were the comments expressed by the recruits indicative of what they really believed and did instructors represent the thoughts of other police officers? Data collection is often dependent on the degree of rapport that the researcher is able to maintain with his subjects. If nobody talks to him, his research is seriously crippled. Hence, the quality of the research depends on the personality of the investigator, his sensitivity to the subtleties of human interaction, his emotional depth and intellectual awareness, his capacity to recognize and counter his own projections, his ability to establish rapport without becoming overidentified and taking things for granted, his awareness of ethical considerations and, above all, his willingness to accept people on their own terms.[11] Indeed, the participatory researcher must consciously cultivate his bias of an

[11] Erik H. Erikson, "The Nature of Clinical Evidence," Daedalus, 87 (1958), pp. 65–87; Frieda Fromm-Reichmann, "On Loneliness," Interpersonal Dynamics, edited by W. G. Bennis et al. (Homewood, Ill.: Dorsey Press, 1964), pp. 715–724; S. M. Miller, "The Participant Observer and 'Over-Rapport,' " American Sociological Review, 17 (1952), pp. 97–99; Maurice S. and Charlotte G. Schwartz, "Problems in Participant Observation," American Journal of Sociology, 60 (1955), pp. 343–353; Arthur J. Vidich, "Participant Observation and the Collection and Interpretation of Data," American Journal of Sociology, 60 (1955), pp. 354–360.

impressionable and receptive mind, which is willing to tolerate, accept and, perhaps, even admire the group for itself, in itself.

Finally, the lack of time and resources plus the necessary sacrifices involved in using one research strategy rather than another have also limited the import of the study. They include the following questions which, in part, remain unanswered. As a case study, can it be generalized to other police training programs? To what degree were the attitudes and behavior of the recruits congruent to the kind of training to which they were exposed? How significant is police training for field work? To what degree and how long do academy influences remain with the recruit once he is in the field? Are personality traits or training forces subordinate to the structural demands of police work? My research strategy may not be able to answer these questions completely, but it lays the foundation for further research that can.

The organization of my data was based on a content analysis of every class lecture, many of the informal recruit discussions, and observations of nonclassroom lessons such as self-defense, pistol shooting, the witnessing of an autopsy, and Field Week. The comments and discussions were all grouped under five topics. One topic covered those conversations relating to past experiences in law enforcement agencies such as Megopolis City Police Department and the military police. These recruits and the recruits who had brothers in various police forces amused themselves and other recruits with humorous and serious anecdotes. The second topic of conversations included reactions to their training at RCPD such as the quality or worth of lectures, instructors, and Field Week experiences. The other three topics of conversation by the recruits referred to either sex, economic concerns, or youthful peccadilloes. These last three topics seemed to identify important bases for police behavior and attitudes that will be presented.

Because most recruit training was spent in a classroom listening to instructors, most of my data are based on this information. A content analysis of the lectures and the few discussions indicates that the academy staff and instructors were preoccupied with certain major concerns. By adopting general perspectives and patterns of behavior from their instructors in response to these concerns, the recruits seemed to become mirror images of their mentors. The concerns of both the instructors and recruits were organized around three themes that seemed to operate on a psychological and a structural level. The themes refer to major problems in police work and also to police responses to these problems. I have labeled these themes as defensiveness, professionalization, and mutual depersonalization. The topics of recruit conversations are integrated within the three themes. Although each theme is discussed separately in the following chapters, in practice, they are intertwined and reinforcing. The theme of defensiveness is discussed first, since it lays the foundation for the other two themes.

I must not have you henceforth question me
Whither I go, nor reason whereabout.
Whither I must, I must; and, to conclude,
This evening must I leave you, gentle Kate.
I know you wise; but yet no farther wise
than Harry Percy's wife. Constant you are,
But yet a woman; and for secrecy,
No lady closer; for I will believe
Thou wilt not utter what thou dost not know;
And so far will I trust thee, gentle Kate.
Shakespeare, I Henry IV

Defensiveness.

CHAPTER THREE

AUTHORITY AND CONTROL

The police officer in American society is in a unique position, since his job is to regulate the behavior of people who do not wish to be regulated. Prison guards and hospital attendants also carry out this function, but they operate in a much more circumscribed territory of action; and in both cases, they regulate persons who have been individually processed by social agencies and declared in need of supervision. The policeman performs his job among the citizenry of his community, who place great value on their constitutionally guaranteed freedom. Furthermore, as a member of the police organization, the officer not only has the authority to control the movement of the citizenry but he is licensed to carry a firearm and intermediate weapons (mace, nightstick, blackjack) and, if necessary, to use them in the course of his duties.

In a democratic society in which individual liberty is highly prized, restraints must be placed on the officer if he is not to intentionally or unintentionally overstep his boundaries of action. It is not uncommon, for instance, for service institutions to become organizationally oriented instead of client oriented. In the case of mental institutions, organizational staff to some extent service themselves and not the patients. Erving Goffman offers some choice examples of the subordination of the needs of the patients to the needs of the organization. In cases in which patients interfered with the smooth functioning of the hospital, the staff dealt with the patient under the guise of concern for his welfare. The solution for promiscuity was hysterectomies; the solution for violent patients was lobotomies; the solution for patients who bit the staff was extractions; the solution for disciplinary problems

27

was shock therapy. The result might have been helpful to the staff, but it was not helping the patient who was supposed to be serviced.

Policemen, too, can easily subordinate the values of a democratic society to their own management problems.[2] The unarmed citizenry carefully scrutinizes the activities of the police organization. Such attempted restraints by the community include a series of court procedures, civil review boards, and exposés through the news media. Finding themselves barraged by a steady onslaught of criticisms from many segments of the community—all of whom the policeman is supposed to be serving—police officers try to protect themselves by curling up individually and organizationally, like the vulnerable porcupine. If anybody or anything outside the department dares attempt to penetrate them with criticisms or with regulating agencies, they let loose quills of anger and indignation. Thus, when New York Mayor John Lindsay attempted to fulfill an election pledge for a police-civilian review board, the city policemen successfully led a movement to defeat his proposal. Not only did they campaign while on duty and in uniform, they also selectively gave traffic tickets to those cars with a pro-review-board bumper sticker.[3]

Most institutions in a modern industrial society are necessarily heavily bureaucratic because of the supposedly efficient character of bureaucracies. The members of the police department structure themselves into a highly bureaucratic organization not only for greater work efficiency but also for greater protection. Authority is centralized, and a chain-of-command is established. Through such a structure, as much control as possible can be exerted over rank-and-file members who cannot be directly supervised in the field. Consequently, the police officer is subject to a system of checks and rechecks that reduces behavioral variations in order to decrease the probability of offending

[1] Erving Goffman, *Asylums* (Garden City, N.Y.: Doubleday, 1961), pp. 348–386. For further examples see Elliot A. Krause, "Functions of a Bureaucratic Ideology: 'Citizen Participation,'" *Social Problems*, 16 (Fall 1968), pp. 129–143; Thomas J. Scheff, *Being Mentally Ill* (Chicago, Ill.: Aldine, 1966); and Edwin M. Schur, *Our Criminal Society* (Englewood Cliffs, N.J.: Prentice-Hall, 1969).

[2] Jerome H. Skolnick, *Justice Without Trial* (New York: John Wiley, 1966); and William A. Westley, "Secrecy and the Police," *Social Forces*, 34 (March 1956), pp. 254–257 and "Violence and the Police," *American Journal of Sociology*, 49 (August 1953), pp. 34–41.

[3] Arthur Niederhoffer, *Behind the Shield* (Garden City, N.Y.: Doubleday, 1967), pp. 170–179. See also, F. K. Heussenstamm, "Bumper Stickers and the Cops," *Trans-Action*, 8 (February 1971), pp. 32–33.

some segment of the community. With so much organizational and psychological energy apparently devoted to protecting themselves and the department, the police organization may be better termed a "defensive bureaucracy." For the purposes of this study, a defensive bureaucracy is a bureaucracy whose members organizationally and individually adjust to their perceptions of hostility, suspicion, or distrust—imagined or real—from the external environment or from the very organization to which they belong.

Perhaps all bureaucracies act defensively toward the external environment, and perhaps all rank-and-file members act defensively toward the organization to some extent. What this concept emphasizes is the interaction between the organization and its environment.[4] For example, one could expect most governmental agencies to be bureaucratic and defensive since, as with the police, they are answerable to the public.

The saliency of defensiveness on an organizational, group, and individual level and its translation to incoming members as they pass through their formal training in a police academy are discussed in the remainder of this chapter.

DEPARTMENTAL CONTROLS AND DEFENSES

The first topic considers the ways in which the police organization tried to assure a maximum of uniform behavior among its members. Essentially three mechanisms were used to achieve this end: laws and rules, written reports, and special squads.

GUIDELINES FOR ACTION

There were two ways in which the recruit appeared to perceive the law. One was as principles of morality, a view that is treated in the

---

[4] Charles Perrow, "Goals in Complex Organizations," *American Sociological Review*, 26 (December 1961), pp. 854–866; Peter Blau et al., "The Structure of Small Democracies," *American Sociological Review*, 31 (April 1966), pp. 179–191; and N. J. Demerath III and Victor Thiessen, "Organizational Precariousness and Irreligion," *American Journal of Sociology*, 71 (May 1966), pp. 674–687.

next chapter. The other was as a set of guidelines for decisions and behavior. These guidelines for action served as a body of rules that the recruit could expect to adhere to if he were to perform his duties effectively and safely. The Good Samaritan Law was presented to the recruit in this way:

> In order to be negligent from not doing something, you must
> have a duty in a special relationship like parent and child; we
> don't have that relationship. . . . You are all going to be sued
> sometime, but I know of no one left out on a limb who sticks to
> the Good Samaritan Law and sticks to the accepted techniques
> of First Aid. So the Samaritan Law protects us if we don't do
> anything, and by the accepted techniques if we do do anything.

However, it became apparent that legal guidelines could provide little help in concrete situations. One instructor recommended that the class not depend too much on the law book. Until a court rules on a concrete case, the laws are too vague. The patrolman, he said, was supposed to know the extent of a person's injuries in order to know the degree of assault to charge an assailant, but how does one define "substantial injury"?

Indeed, the recruit discovered legal ambiguities for himself. During a lecture on larceny (one that had been presented to recruits and officers for years), the class pointed out to the instructor that according to the law, larceny second degree and larceny third degree overlapped. The instructor called up the county seat and spoke to the district attorney and three assistant district attorneys. When he returned to the class, he admitted that he could not provide a definite answer. Two of the officials had said one thing, and two another.

To help the policeman operate within a system of vague laws that would require him to use his own discretion and leave his judgment open to question, the department established its own rules and procedures. Since the courts evaluated an officer's actions according to his conformity to or variation from departmental policy, the rules and procedures became tantamount to law. If an officer deviated from standard procedures, he opened himself up to civil suits, departmental discipline, or criminal prosecution. As long as the officer operated within the department's rules and procedures, neither he nor the department could be charged with corruption or incompetence. Nowhere was this more apparent than in the instruction the recruit received in first aid.

> There may be situations where there is more than one
> emergency. You have to decide on whom to start on first [e.g.,
> a bleeding victim takes precedence over a non-breathing victim].

This is where we have priorities, and to assist you in who or what to begin with, we have set up a list of priorities to decide for you. Our intention here is to reduce it to as little decision making as possible. . . . As long as you follow the guidelines, no one can touch you in any law suit.

If departmental rules and procedures were intended to aid the officer in performing his duties within a system of ambiguous laws, the recruit did not seem to interpret them that way. As James Q. Wilson observes, the numerous rules of a police department usually instructed the officer on what he could not do, not on what he could do.[5] To the recruit, the rules seemed to indicate that he was essentially distrusted by the public and, perhaps, even by his own department. Some rules were particularly gnawing. For instance, if an officer wrote a report on lost or stolen jewelry, he was not allowed to describe the items in terms of gold, silver, ruby, and so forth. "No police officer is considered a jeweler," so he must describe the items as yellow metal, white metal, or red glass. In this case, the department was trying to protect the officer from being ridiculed by a defense attorney or from being embarrassed if the "victim" reported a stolen diamond which was really glass. Nevertheless, regulations for such a "trivial" matter seemed insulting to the recruit and challenged his image of himself as a competent and skilled worker. These apparent attitudes came into sharp focus during one rare argument in class regarding the selection of tow trucks at the scene of an automobile accident.

Before the county police department was established in 1960, there was a town scandal involving allegations that police officers were receiving kickbacks from towers who were called to the scene. As a result, town ordinances were passed that forced the police officer to select a town-licensed tower from a list in proper order. The recruit seemed to balk at this restriction. He seemed to define the ordinances as unfair and contrary to his professional status as someone capable of making independent decisions. He also seemed to identify with the victims, for almost every recruit had been involved in, at least, one accident and was aware of the high costs of towing.

[5] James Q. Wilson, *Varieties of Police Behavior* (Cambridge, Mass.: Harvard University Press, 1968), pp. 74–77.

R₁: What if I lived in Oakville and the tower is from Springdale, I have to have it towed to Springdale?

I: Yes. Look, you're thinking like Joe Citizen. You can't think like Joe Citizen. You *must* do this by town ordinance.

R₂: But we have to explain it to Joe Citizen.

I: You have no choice. Let him fight with town hall. It's not our responsibility.

R₃: Sir, I'm a professional police officer. There's a two-lane accident, a tower on the list is right there at the scene, but it's not his turn.

I: No, he must wait until his turn comes up.

Rs: We're going to have to make collars [arrests] at every accident!

Other evidence seemed to define the recruit and patrolman as untrustworthy. For instance, if a recruit or member of the department reported his absence due to sickness, the rules required an on-duty officer to check on him at his home. An instructor warned the recruit that he had better not be painting when the on-duty officer arrived at his home. If the absentee was not at home because of a doctor's appointment, "have the doctor's slip ready."

An officer had to protect himself if he ever had occasion to enter a bar or liquor store—either by having a witness with him or by entering the time and length of stay into his notebook. The assumption was that if he did not write the matter into his memo book, he had something to hide. The liquor business was the only area in which an officer definitely was not allowed to hold a second job because of its historical underworld connections. If he had any financial interest in a liquor-related business, directly or indirectly, he had to sell it before he joined the department.

The recruit was also warned not to try to get away with using mace for unofficial reasons. The can of mace was weighed periodically and the number of squirts used was calculated. The calculation was then checked against the patrolman's reports of how many times he had used his mace. If there was any discrepancy, the patrolmen would have to explain it. "What are you going to say, 'I was practicing in the basement'?"

Although the rules may have indicated to the recruit that he was distrusted by the department, the department had to protect itself from adverse publicity as much as possible. In doing so, it tried to clamp down on the amount of discretion available to its members as they operated within ambiguous laws.[6] Although many rules did, in fact, protect the officer from suits and complaints, the recruit appeared to take these restrictions personally. On the one hand, he was told he was a professional, which conveyed a sense of individual competence that should go unquestioned. On the other hand, he was subject to detailed rules. Consequently, the rules and procedures intended to protect the officer were perceived by the recruit as another body of rules from which he would have to protect himself in the course of his duties.

THE REPORTING SYSTEM

One of the most effective protective devices used by the department was a complex and cumbersome system of checks and rechecks of police activities through written reports. Each officer had to carry a memo book as part of his daily equipment. In it he wrote the day, the hours of his shift, the weather, when he reported on and off duty, where and when he lunched or relieved himself, the time and description of every police call to which he responded, and brief notations of anything out of the ordinary. At the end of his tour, he had to sign his name on the very next open line on the page to prevent his adding (or being charged with adding) something at a later date. The responsibility for the accuracy of the memo book was shared by his field sergeant who was required to countersign the day's report. This, of course, enabled administrative officers to control the field sergeant: if his countersignature is not found on each daily report of each member of his squad, he must not be supervising his men properly.

For every police-involved incident, the officer also had to write up a field report in as many copies as were required for a particular incident: automobile accident, drunken driving, arrests (a supple-

---

[6] Using Alvin Gouldner's exposition of a punishment-centered bureaucracy, John H. McNamara suggests another function of the rules and procedures of police departments. Managers of a punishment-centered bureaucracy assume worker nonconformity is a result of willful intent rather than of poor judgment or ignorance. Consequently, management formalizes many rules to clearly warn the worker of its expectations of him and to justify any punishment if those expectations are not met. "Uncertainties in Police Work: The Relevance of Police Recruits' Backgrounds and Training," *The Police*, edited by David J. Bordua (New York: John Wiley, 1967), pp. 178–186. See also Gouldner's *Patterns of Industrial Bureaucracy* (Glencoe, Ill.: Free Press, 1954), pp. 168–172.

mental form if physical force was used during an arrest), impounded cars, stolen cars, keeping and transferring evidence, holding property, ad infinitum, ad nauseum. These reports, too, had to be checked by the field sergeant and possibly by the on-duty lieutenant. Unlike the medical student, who is also fearful of making mistakes in his reports that could result in possible law suits, the police officer is subject to several supervisory steps—no matter how much experience he has.[7]

The instructors told the recruit that this was all for his protection. According to several instructors, the memo book and field reports were:

> . . . most important. It's your diary, and if a field report is missing,
> you'll have to make out another. Always fill out the field
> report . . . It is your personal business record, nobody else's.
> You and I know one of the first duties of the sergeant is to check
> your memo book and sign it. But use it only as a business record.
> If a sergeant sees a personal entry, you'll hear about it. You'll
> be at the wailing wall a long time.

In addition to its function of restraining the independent action of the officer, the reporting system provided data that the department could use to back up its requests for higher budgets and more personnel during its annual battle with an external regulating agency, the County Board of Supervisors. The daily field reports were coded and transferred to computer cards to construct statistical information. One instructor recognized the manipulative and protective roles of statistical reports that could demonstrate to the community the efficiency of the department.[8] He advised the recruits to

> [c]harge him with the greater offense, although members of the
> Civil Liberties Union may misconstrue this, so if he gets off the
> more serious one, you can get him on a lesser charge. This is
> what "copping the plea" is. Maybe it's justly criticized, but it
> makes the records look good.

As Blumberg forcefully argues, the entire criminal justice system is characterized by efficiency, smoothness, and the mediocrity of assembly-line justice. The care spent by the police in filing reports is only part of the constellation. Judges, district attorneys, prison offi-

---

[7] Howard S. Becker et al., *Boys in White* (Chicago: University of Chicago Press, 1961).
[8] See Jerome H. Skolnick, pp. 164–181, Edwin M. Schur, *Our Criminal Society*, pp. 23–54, and Abraham S. Blumberg, *Criminal Justice* (Chicago, Ill.: Quadrangle, 1967), for further and broader implications of clearance rates.

cials, and police are apt to focus on making themselves look good on paper: all replace the goal of due process and justice with administrative convenience.

Several times instructors urged neat, concise, and complete reports because they were an important criterion for promotion. If he wrote sloppily or shoddily, the recruit was warned, he should not expect to be promoted to sergeant or detective. Spelling should be accurate so as not to provide a defense counsel with an opportunity to discredit the officer.

> Be legible; print if you have to. Don't abbreviate; avoid erasures—
> in any form. Just draw a line through it. That's the way an auditor
> corrects his books. You show you haven't hidden anything. You
> wait till a defense lawyer sees an erasure. He'll make you feel
> so high, no matter what your intentions were.

By the end of the training session, one recruit (after being told that any summons issued by a patrolman must be sworn to in front of the desk sergeant) remarked despondently, "You feel like you're not trusted all the way down the line."

It seemed, then, that the check-recheck reporting system was not so much for the officer's individual protection (as the instructors claimed) as it was a device to protect the department from complaints of inefficiency or from possible law suits. How could the punitive measures taken by the department be otherwise explained when the memo book did not meet certain standards? If the reporting system had been for the officer's personal protection alone, it would not have appeared so aggravating to, and a cause of anxiety for, the recruit. Apparently, the network of written reports provided a rough check on the activities of departmental rank-and-file members, backed up requests made of the county, provided a record of events in case of charges of incompetence or inaction, and increased the likelihood of a conviction (if the reports were accurate)—all of which suggests the extent to which the network was organizationally oriented.

GROUP DEFENSES

The structural protective mechanisms went beyond the bureaucratic patterns of behavior and the reporting system that were basically intraorganizational controls. The police department formed official squads to present their points of view to the community or to counter those of out-groups. One such squad was the Community Relations Squad. Its purposes were to reduce police-community friction, to foster mutual understanding, and to defend police actions from external criticisms.

On the recruit-patrolman level at least, it seemed as if community relations were perceived as a problem of the community. The police officer was merely trying to do the job that he was sworn to do; if there was to be any change in relations, it had to be on the part of the community. Thus, the recruit was evading police-community problems and ambiguities by defining them as basically the community's problem.[9] This was quite obvious when, after the training session ended, I was invited to sit in on an in-service training program for patrolmen that was dealing with police-youth problems.

A panel was made up of five youths: two blacks with police records, a high school champion athlete, a vice-president of a high school council, and a leader of a teen-age group. A lieutenant of the Community Relations Squad was the moderator. It was my opinion that only the youngsters tried to stick to the topic of police and teen-age relations. Whenever a youngster tried to get the discussion back on track (particularly the vice-president), the lieutenant reduced the complaint to a problem that stemmed from the community, not from the police. It seemed as if he was trying to show the patrolmen in the class that the squad was really working for their interests. On the other hand, the patrolmen seemed more concerned about proving that the criticisms against the police were unfounded than with trying to understand the points of view of the youngsters. This defensive nature of Community Relations was explicitly stated to the recruit class by an instructor.

> We have Community Relations because the people are more
> educated than they were before. They also complain more. So the
> only way we defend ourselves is more awareness of the need of
> police-community relations techniques. We can't survive in
> today's society if we are just a punishing or law enforcing agency.

In one Community Relations seminar, however, the recruit learned to perceive this squad as just another department mechanism of defense, on which he, as an individual, could not depend. The leader of our seminar related a story about a store owner who constantly called up headquarters to complain that the police did not patrol his area enough. If a patrol car was not immediately forthcoming, he

---

[9] Rose Laub Coser, "Evasiveness as a Response to Structural Ambivalence," *Social Science and Medicine*, 1 (1967), pp. 203–218.

would telephone to complain again. One time the assigned patrolman was unable to respond because he had been snowed under with the paper work of a bad car accident. The seminar leader was asked to handle the complaint. According to him, he told the irate store owner that he would check out why the officer never responded to his call. He then went around the corner, had some coffee, and returned. He promised the store owner that he, the department, and the commissioner guaranteed that an incident of this kind would never again occur. The store owner reacted by becoming meek—he did not want to get anybody in trouble, he just wanted to know why a patrol car never came. From then on, said the instructor, he never complained to the department again. The recruit's reactions were immediate.

R₁: I would never do that. You're doing community relations
    by busting the balls of a fellow officer!

CR: Right away you're being defensive.

R₂: No, I'd tell him the truth, that the officer was at a car accident
    snowed under papers all night.

R₁: I would never make a scapegoat of a brother officer because,
    baby, he's tops!

CR: (unconvincingly) Well, if this really happened, I wouldn't
    be here if I stomped fellow cops. But I wanted to see how
    you'd react to the story.

While the Community Relations Squad was the unit that tried to explain the department's perspective to out-groups, the Inspection Squad operated within the in-group. Inspection investigated complaints made against the department and otherwise saw to it that departmental standards were maintained: it policed the police. But it, too, appeared to be a mechanism for defense against the community. The recruit was told:

We have the Inspection Squad to handle all complaints against
the department. We have to police ourselves, or they'll come in
and police in place of us. For a while Megopolis City had a
Civilian Review Board; their excuse was the police department
wasn't policing itself. Most of the time the complaints are found
to be unbased. We have to go through the mechanics. We have
to look into all the complaints. You have to go before Inspection.

Regarding the necessity of using "deadly physical force" (firearms) in the course of his work, the recruit was informed that, "sometimes we do have hearings to let the public know there are safeguards."

In effect, the hearings were used by the department so that it would look good in the eyes of the community, and the recruit felt even more threatened.

As if that were not enough, the recruit class found out from an instructor that all citizen complaints about an officer remained in his permanent file whether or not a trial proved the accusations unfounded. Here, the instructor was unable to justify the departmental position to the satisfaction of the recruit. This further confirmed the recruit's apparent feeling that he could not depend on the department in the last analysis. During lunch, one recruit expressed the thoughts of most of the others: "They say they are going to protect you. Ha! I don't want that kind of protection."

With the department so intent on maintaining harmonious relations with the community, the individual recruit felt that he was in a precarious position. He believed that if he or any other officer were ever brought up on charges, the officer would be found guilty regardless of the evidence in order to placate the public.[10] Although there were various responses he could make as an individual, such as never informing on a brother officer or going "by the book," the officer tended to find security in a formal group composed of men like himself. The Police Association, the Police Conference, and the Police Brotherhood Association were three such organizations comprised mostly of rank-and-file men—the men on the beat.

These organizations protected the officer from community abuse and also from possible "arbitrary" decisions (those detrimental to the patrolman) by the department, even to the extent of providing him with a lawyer if a formal charge were made against him. The recruit was further encouraged to join PBA because of its interest in higher salaries, increased medical and dental benefits, improved life insurance programs, and because it would increase the power of the police lobby in the state legislature.

The sense of solidarity fostered through these groups provided the officer with considerable moral support as he performed his work. Without the confidence of knowing that someone is always ready to help him in dangerous or sticky situations, the officer would probably hesitate to act at all. In remarking about his own lack of training, an instructor informed the recruit about departmental solidarity.

In this department you're backed to the hilt. It's a good feeling

---

[10] James Q. Wilson, pp. 75–76, and Arthur Niederhoffer, p. 173.

knowing someone is there behind you. One time I had to go into
a restaurant to arrest an obscene caller. I was scared, but I went
in with my hand on my gun. A patrol car happened to come by
there. Nothing happened, but it's nice when a guy comes to
help out.

Another instructor put it more powerfully. "The car radio is powerful.
You call a 10–1 officer in need of help and, by God, you'll have the
whole police department behind you."

TERRITORY OF ACTION

Implicit in the content of academy training was an awareness of
temporal and spatial territories of action in which the recruit had to
operate as a patrolman. His responsibilities lay within these territorial boundaries, and these responsibilities seemed to contribute to
the recruit's sense of vulnerability to forces beyond his control.

A patrolman should confine his activities to his territorial sector
during his eight-hour tour of duty.[11] Except for circumstances in which
a brother officer needed help, the recruit was instructed to stick to his
sector and "keep your nose clean." Once he was assigned to a sector,
it was the officer's responsibility to familiarize himself with its houses
and buildings. He should check furnaces and stoves and note fire
escapes and exits. He should also become acquainted with the people
who live or work in his sector. He was told that someday a detective
was going to describe someone to him, "so you better be able to
identify who he is."

Territoriality included the safety of one's own person and equipment. The instructors advised the recruit on how to protect himself
from possible dangers on and off the job. Not only was the officer
responsible for his own safety, he was responsible for the safety of
those citizens with whom he came into contact. For example, in covering an automobile accident, he should keep the operators in sight at
all times even if they look fine. The officer was also responsible for a
citizen's property if the latter were a victim of an accident. During one

---

[11] Arthur L. Stinchcombe, "Institutions of Privacy in the Determination of Police Administration Practice," *American Journal of Sociology*, 69 (September 1963), pp. 150–160,
points out the difference between rural and urban territories of action for the police
officer.

lecture, the recruit appeared to become concerned about this responsibility—which was in addition to his having to care for injured parties and having to fill out field reports and accident forms. The officer was still held responsible for valuables in the victim's car because the injured party cannot be responsible himself. "It all falls back on you."

Yet, the recruit seemed to realize that the victim's property had to be protected by someone. A group of recruits discussed several instances in which they knew of a victim who had been robbed while he was unconscious from a car accident. Some of the stories involved a policeman's doing the stealing. It just seemed to the recruit that he was held responsible for so much that he could easily overlook something for which he could be reprimanded.

Since there had to be a record of events of each patrolman's daily tour of duty, records were also a part of his territory. He was responsible for every official article he received from another officer and for obtaining signatures that certified when and from whom he received it and when and to whom he passed it on. This connected chain of signatures with dates had to be maintained if it related to the evidence of a crime or it would not be admissible in court. An historical record of warrants was also important for two reasons: (1) so that the warrant would not be lost; and (2) so that the department would not be left open to suits for false arrests, in case a copy of the warrant had already been served on the same person. Warrants used to be photocopied until two warrants were served on the same person and cost the county $50,000.

The officer's territory of action was also delimited in terms of time. An instructor half seriously and half jokingly referred to the patrolman's apparent inclination to remain uninvolved in a case shortly before the end of his tour of duty.

> The biggest thing in citizen arrests is arbitration. You're the guy
> in the middle. Arbitration is the biggest thing—especially if it's
> ten minutes before your relief!

For the recruit, time appeared to have another dimension. His first goal was to graduate from the academy after three months of training, but he also had to last nine more months in the field, during which time he could easily be dismissed. An instructor put it this way:

> Now if you're sick before the end of your one year probation and
> you're not well by that time, you're out and have to start with
> civil service again. Or you can get well before the year is up,
> or you can resign and then reapply for active duty. Get that year
> under your belt for security. You're neither fish nor fowl.

The last component of the policeman's territory of action seemed to include his family. Unlike most occupations, the police officer literally brought his work home with him. This did not necessarily mean he talked to his wife about his job; some recruits took care to segregate their work from their family as much as possible. He did, however, bring some of his equipment home, which added to the family's danger and caused a nagging subterranean fear that someone might have an accident with his weapons.

The instructors urged the recruit to abide by their safety standards to protect himself and his family. He was advised to keep his revolver unloaded, to handcuff the cylinder or the finger guard open, to store it on the highest shelf in the home, and to store the ammunition in a separate place. He should also take care about hiding his can of mace in case the children think "mommy has a new hairspray." The point was graphically supported at the medical examiner's office. Before the recruit witnessed an autopsy, he was desensitized to looking at dead bodies by seeing slides of bodies in various states of death from various causes. One of the slides was of a man who had been shot by his wife; she had killed him with her (police officer) son's revolver.

The recruit might cross his territorial boundaries, but his instructors advised him that it would be safer not to. One instructor suggested that he not extend his territory to times when he was with his family, for example, during a weekend drive: "Mind your own business. You get in more trouble when you are in your own car. Just think of your wife and children before you do anything."

The department recognized the impact of its members' occupation on their families. Before the recruit was accepted into the department, his background investigation included an interview with his wife. The investigators made sure the wife understood what adjustments were necessary as her husband rotated shifts each week, what it meant to have firearms in the house with children, and what consequences they might have for childrearing. The commissioner, too, recognized the importance of the family unit in police work. Before and during the graduation ceremony, he indicated that the ceremony was a family affair; when a recruit joined the department, he brought his family with him.

Throughout the academy training, the recruit appeared to be impressed that not only did he bring his family into physical danger by virtue of his occupation, he opened them up to financial dangers as well. He was, or felt he was, highly vulnerable to law suits regardless of the honesty of his mistakes. The staff tried to lessen the anxiety of the recruit by explaining that as far as the department was concerned, no officer was culpable for an honest mistake. This might have relieved the recruit's concern about departmental discipline some-what, but it provided little comfort regarding citizen-initiated suits. The only "encouraging" advice one instructor offered was:

> In your twenty years you'll be sued. You're looking at a man who is in a $500,000 suit. You'll be sued too. Whether they collect is another question.

Such a statement did little to bolster the recruit's confidence. Indeed, by the end of the second week, the recruit had learned so many ways he could make an error in arrests that he seemed to feel that it was impossible for him to act without opening himself to a legal suit. Thus it seemed a better alternative to underenforce the law than to enforce it fully. Of course, underenforcing the law has psychological dangers, as Arthur E. Hippler notes. Police inactivity tends to lead to frustration and low self-esteem, which can lead to outbursts of police over-reaction and violence in situations calling for calm and deliberation.[12]

The recruit learned that the very people who request his service might turn on him at a later day. He was taught to be distrustful of others and to protect himself in as many ways as possible. In the case of a family disturbance complaint in which the wife demanded that the officer arrest her husband, an instructor warned that the recruit should have her sign a statement that she requested the arrest. If he does not get the signature, and if she does not go to the station house in the morning to sign the complaint, he can be sued for false arrest. Also, if the recruit had to impound a car, he was cautioned to care-fully note the condition of the vehicle on the proper form because "they'll try to blame you for the dent in the fender." Otherwise, he could easily find himself in a law suit and subject to departmental discipline.

This sense of vulnerability to legal suits and departmental discipline in the performance of his duty appeared to contribute a great deal to the recruit's apparent hesitancy to act. It seemed safer to remain uninvolved. Yet it was difficult to teach him otherwise, for he was, indeed, vulnerable. If he were not aware of the tricks people could play on him at his expense, he could find himself in jail or with a bond placed on his paycheck. The recruit had to learn to protect himself and the department from law suits, but he was also expected to

---

[12] Arthur E. Hippler, "The Game of Black and White at Hunters Point," *Trans-Action*, 7 (April 1970), p. 58.

enforce the law boldly. How the individual recruit and patrolman reacted to this dilemma will be examined later in this chapter.

ETHOS OF DEFENSIVENESS

The recruit learned that there was more to worry about than just detailed reports and memo books, legal suits, or dangers to his family. For instance, out of the routine he realized that he might lose his life or a limb. He learned about the duplicity of community spokesmen and the public at large in their relationships with him. In addition, he encountered evidence that his enemies were within the department as well as outside of it. He soon came to expect that his actions would be continuously watched by someone "out to get him." How the recruit acquired these apparent definitions is the major concern of this rather lengthy portion of the discussion on defensiveness.

THE UNPREDICTABLE ROUTINE

So that he would be prepared for the "one time it counts," the recruit was constantly reminded to rigorously conform to the department's rules and procedures. Out of the routine came the unexpected. He must never look on the routine routinely; nothing must be taken for granted. At the precise moment that he relaxed his guard, he might lose his life. Family altercation calls were considered to be dangerous calls because there was no way of knowing what would happen. The story was told about a sergeant who responded to a family altercation call. Instead of responding cautiously, he parked in front of the house and walked the 60 or so feet to the front door. He was paralyzed for life. He had been shot by the resident, a drunken Megopolis City policeman.

During classes led by an FBI agent, several short films of police procedure were shown. Each film was a lesson in how the routine stop, the routine search, or the routine arrest could well result in the officer's death because of one careless mistake. An officer had to be on the alert constantly.[13] In one scene, a state policeman stopped a

---

[13] Erving Goffman, "Where the Action Is," *Interaction Ritual* (Chicago: Aldine, 1967), esp. pp. 170–174, discusses danger as a life-style.

car for a routine check of the occupant's license and registration. The officer followed the procedures properly and the driver was courteous —until the officer turned in such a way that his holster was exposed to the driver. The driver grabbed the revolver, killed the officer, and ran across the nearby field. He happened to be an escaped mental patient.

In another scene, a policeman stopped a speeding convertible that was driven by a blonde, apparently the only occupant of the car. As the smiling officer walked up to her door, a man jumped up from the floor of the back seat and killed him with a revolver. The lesson here was that an officer should always check the contents of the back seat with his gun hand ready before he walks up to the front door. The film's commentator ended with: "Walker made one mistake, and it cost him his life. You must make suspicion a condition of habit; it must be first nature. Walker thought he made a routine stop."

At the coffee break following the films, the recruits presented mixed attitudes toward the dangers of their work routine.

R_1:　Look, if someone jumps up out of a car at you, you're dead,
　　　　that's all there is to it.

R_2:　We have the "Rules and Procedures." That guy in the film
　　　　wouldn't have been killed if he had done what the rules said.
　　　　He would have looked in the back seat instead of walking
　　　　up to the girl.

R_3:　There's nothing you can do about it. If you saw a person lying
　　　　in the back seat, your first instinct is to figure he's sick,
　　　　not to jump up with a drawn gun. That's the name of the game.

R_2:　I still say, all you have to do is follow the "Rules and Procedures."

R_4:　Well, let's take Watts for instance. A Negro walks up to a cop
　　　　and says, "Sir, there's trouble down the street," and then
　　　　he pulls out a shotgun and starts firing. The cop got under
　　　　the car, but across the street more guys are firing .45's.
　　　　There's no defense for that. You've had it.

Being prepared for the unexpected or the "one in a thousandth" time was encouraged, not only for the personal safety of the officer but also for the proper enforcement of the law. The recruit was instructed to write down anything that seemed unusual in his memo book, for what had seemed insignificant at one time might later become the means of breaking a case. He was taught that the one good entry "far outweighs the time and effort used in making numerous unproductive notations." All rumors, no matter how trivial, should be reported and checked out. Like the notations in the memo book, the one time it counted, more than compensated for the hours of drudgery—at least, that was what the instructors suggested.

It was the unpredictable thousandth and one time that seemed to be impressed upon the recruit. The other thousand times were practice sessions for the "real thing."

> One thing I have to mention is the need to have your weapons
> at all times. When we were a bit lax, one man left the station
> saying he was just going around the corner for some cigarettes
> and walked in the middle of a hold-up. He didn't have his
> weapon, and it doesn't look good. You can always go out with
> your gun a thousand times, but it's always the thousandth and
> one time when you forget it.

Like the professional boxer, the police officer must constantly be prepared for the time when he will be "summoned to fight."[14] He was warned that he must "get into good physical fitness and stay in it, because you never know when you need to react quickly and with strength." To become lax in even the insignificant routine of daily patrol might result in personal injury or missing an opportunity to enforce the law. In the academy, the recruit was prepared for emergencies (such as riots or crime searches with which the recruit class might be asked to help) by unannounced inspections, "so get in the habit; we don't want you caught short."

In addition to preparing for the "one that counts," the recruit also learned that he must survive tasks for which he did not have a thousand dry runs, or any practice at all. He was alerted to other dangers of his job for which it would be hard to prepare. For example, the recruit was encouraged to adopt a hobby that would keep him in good physical condition. Riots take their toll physically and mentally, and "these professional agitators, they know what words raise this emotion with this idea in mind."

Because he carried firearms on and off duty, the officer was constantly aware of the possibilities of accidents occurring. The staff and firearms instructors emphasized the precautions the recruit should take for his own safety. But each warning added just one more thing for the recruit to worry about that had consequences for his personal safety.

---

[14] S. Kirson Weinberg and Henry Arond, "The Occupational Culture of the Boxer," *American Journal of Sociology*, 63 (March 1952), pp. 460–469.

Check the ejector rod periodically also, so it doesn't jam and you can't open the chamber. Check all screws. The strain screw balances the hammer. If it comes loose, it can cause misfiring. Don't ever let oil get on your primer. Oil will kill the primer in nothing flat.

Never use a trigger shoe outside the range. We've had a man shoot himself . . . because it extends beyond the trigger guard. Another killed his wife when he was cleaning it. One man was killed because he couldn't shoot because the shoe caught.

You'll hear from the experienced men to remove all the moving parts because it's easier. But they don't tell you it can become unsafe. For example, without a safety bar, a gun can fire if it's dropped. So don't ever say you shot a person when you dropped your gun. . . .

If you drop a weapon, don't put it back in your holster. Have it checked out. If you close your weapon with a flick of the wrist, it looks good, but it knocks hell out of the alignment. Leave it to Humphrey Bogart.

Never, ever take it for granted a firearm is unloaded. And check to see if it is reloaded when you go on duty. If you find your hammer open when it's in the holster, get your finger between the hammer and the frame, pull the trigger, easing off the hammer, then release the trigger, ease the hammer down to get the safety bar up there. Learn this. [Repeats process three times slowly.] Sooner or later you'll get your gun entangled.

Don't telegraph your firearms to a prisoner. At courts where there's a crowd, keep your hand on the handle. Protect that gun!

Another source of worry to the recruit was the possibility of catching diseases from derelicts or dead bodies, which he had to touch in the course of his work. One recruit who came from the Megopolis Department said he carried a pair of gloves for these situations. Some of the instructors, such as the medical examiner and the first aid instructor, tried to dispel these fears. The recruit was informed that the chance of catching something from a body was practically nil, since the body fights off the major communicable diseases everyday. The only exception was jaundiced bodies.

Nevertheless, the recruit remained worried. It was the "practically nil" idea with which he had been bombarded throughout his training. He had heard stories from his police friends that he could catch anything from sick or dead persons. Being told to wash his hands anytime that he made an arrest for LSD confirmed any doubts he might have had. A lecturer from the Narcotics Squad mentioned that after 15 minutes of ingestion of LSD there was nothing that could be done about it. "Just the stuff that may be on your fingers would be enough."

OUT-GROUPS

Specific groups within the community added to the recruit's sense of defensiveness. He seemed unable to understand why the people he was trying to serve did not appear to appreciate his efforts or sacrifices. It was as if these groups were mobilized specifically to make his task harder, and to make the criminal's ability to circumvent the law that much easier. There seemed to be eight major out-groups that the recruit perceived as interfering with police work and police goals. These were the groups that the police had to continually contend with in their efforts to enforce the law. The six groups to be discussed in this section are: politicians, students, blacks (representing colored minority groups), newsmen, females, and the amorphous public of which the preceding groups are a part. The other two groups, lawyers and judges, will be discussed in the next chapter. Each group was seen as an out-group, although individuals within these groups might vary with respect to their sympathy and support of police actions.

POLITICIANS. The politicians comprised an out-group because they appeared unwilling to support the police in controversial matters if it was politically expedient not to do so. The recruit seemed to regard himself as the scapegoat for political maneuvers. Once, the class complained to a lecturer that during riots the politicians should go down and hear the complaints of the rioters, since they were the ones who made the promises. "We're always left holding the bag."

Politicians were also likely to make unwise decisions regarding police affairs. One instructor complained that police problems were often a result of nonpolice personnel making the final decisions. For example, during a budgetary battle with the Town Board of Supervisors, a $3000 piece of equipment was approved, while a $60 item was rejected. Yet the expensive item remained in storage because the other item was necessary for its use.

If politicians constituted an out-group, liberal politicians were an "outer-group." They were believed to be misinformed people at best and, perhaps, even part of a conspiracy to undermine basic American values at worst. At the time of the research, there was a proposal initiated by a "liberal" mayor for his city police department that was of great concern to police officials across the nation. Police departments are generally based on a three platoon per day system: one works an 8:00 A.M. to 4:00 P.M. shift, another the 4:00 P.M. to 12:00 A.M. shift, and a third the 12:00 A.M. to 8:00 A.M. shift. Thus, three platoons operate within every 24 hours. The mayor proposed that a fourth platoon be created to patrol in conjunction with tours of duty during the high crime hours, 6:00 P.M. to 2:00 A.M.

One instructor tried to show the stupidity of this "typically liberal" proposal.

> That mayor says, "We have the biggest increase in crime between the hours of six and two." So he says, "We'll have four platoons instead of three." Hey, their State law says each department should only have three platoons. So he says, "We'll change the law." So this is how he solves the problems—by manpower. So someone asks, "Why by manpower?" "Because they'll see the cop and won't do anything." Then some real smart guy asks, "For what kind of crimes and where?" ... So we check the records and find that 40% of the rapes are only on the street. The others were in other places like apartments and parks. How does manpower take care of the other 60%?

At lunch a recruit laughed,

> It seems they always have to bring something up every now and then to stir up the people. They'll never pass it. They tried to pass the name tags and it lasted three days. They'll never pass it.

For this recruit it would be merely a matter of waiting out these liberal proposals until their "stupidity" was demonstrated in practice.

STUDENTS. In the beginning of the training session, the instructors showed the recruit that even with his own lack of education he was superior to college students.

> I hear in our institutions of higher learning they filled up a trash can with crap, and then they crapped all over the floor. They were asked why they crapped on the rug, they said, "Man, there ain't no more room in the waste basket." (Laughter) These are supposed to be educated people!

Soon, however, the emphasis changed from viewing the students as a comparison group composed of morally inferior people to viewing them as an out-group hostile to the principles of law and order.

> They hate cops, they hate law and order, they hate the uniform. This is not to say you have to be nice with them because what they need is a good kick in the pants, but be courteous. We can't take them out and kick them in the balls. Today we have to use professionalization.

Several derogatory references were made about college students by the recruits during the training session. But not until my lecture and the ensuing debate shortly before the end of the session did they fully express their sentiments. College students, they claimed, had no respect for the law and felt they could break it with impunity. Campus demonstrations involved a small minority of students whose sole aim was to disrupt classes to express minority causes. Other students were motivated to join them merely from the desire to be "one of the gang." Their promiscuous behavior, style of dress, and general rejection of middle class morality was further evidence of their decadence. All of these patterns of behavior could be explained by one factor: they were spoiled as children—in spite of the overwhelming evidence that persons who commit crimes of violence tend to come from unpermissive families! Students never had to work for a living while "we had to bust our humps to get the things we got." The instructors seemed to agree with this convenient but oversimplified explanation, for nothing was done to dispel these beliefs. If anything, they were confirmed.

BLACKS. Recruit attitudes about blacks and other colored minority groups (Mexican Americans, Cubans, Puerto Ricans) seemed to be based on two intertwined factors: (1) their perceived criminal threat as reflected in their high rates of arrests as compared to other ethnic groups, and (2) their perceived denial of the work ethic as reflected in their high rates of welfare recipients. As far as the recruit seemed to be concerned, if a man was on welfare, he must be lazy; if a woman was on welfare, she must be promiscuous. This belief appeared to be based on the recruit's knowledge of the various ploys some welfare recipients used in order to claim more money than they deserved: giving birth to more children, using two different names, or claiming dependency while living with a spouse. When the recruit heard about welfare people's demand for Christmas subsidies, he seemed indignant. "They already have free medical and dental care, and they want money to spend on luxuries now!" Such a condition seemed unfair to a person who was struggling to make his own way in life.

During a class in which the welfare question was discussed, a recruit asked resentfully:

Sir, what about when welfare becomes a way of life? One woman from Mississippi had twelve little bastards and gets $750 a month, tax free. Her sole purpose was to get welfare checks in [state].

The recruit's attitudes seemed to harden as he realized that areas of high welfare subsidies also tended to be areas of high crime. The black seemed to be defined as a potential criminal (unless he had made it to the middle class), who became an actual criminal when the opportunity occurred.[15] The looting during riots was only one such example. Black organizations appeared to be antipolice, whose sole purpose was to earn their members more latitude in breaking the law by challenging the legality of police behavior if one of their group was arrested. The recruit was perplexed over this disparity of law enforcement expectations. He believed that while a white would expect to get shot at if he were fleeing from a crime, a black would cry police brutality and expect to get away with his crime. These groups, supported by liberal politicians and students or those who let themselves be intimidated by them, seemed to want freedom from all law, not justice or equality. One recruit from Megopolis Department mentioned in class that he was ordered by his superiors never to get involved with giving a black a traffic violation summons. This reverse discrimination appeared to reinforce the already well-paved hostility against blacks.

THE PRESS. With the exception of lawyers, there appeared to be no other group considered as deceitful as newsmen. While lawyers distorted the law, the press distorted the news. Although it was the commissioner's policy to present all the available information about a police situation to the press, even if it might be detrimental to the interests of the department, the recruit seemed skeptical as to his fairness, since the press would be sure to distort the information anyway.[16] Early in the training session, the recruit was warned about newsmen.

> A reporter's story is made on what you don't tell them, not on what you tell them. That's what they're paid for. . . . Never trust the press. They bait you. All you have to do is say something, and they wrap it around your neck.

[15] William A. Westley observes the same definitions working in his department, *Violence and the Police* (Cambridge, Mass.: MIT Press, 1970), pp. 99–105. See also Arthur E. Hippler, pp. 58–59.

[16] Benjamin Stalzer, "Press Portrayal of the New York City Police Department with a Content Analysis of the New York *Daily News* and the New York *Times* of April 1, 1958 to October 1, 1958" (unpublished Master's thesis), New York City College, Bernard M. Baruch School of Business and Public Administration, 1961, reports that the news actually favors the police.

The recruit clicked his tongue in disgust each time the instructor who lectured on police-press relations pointed out an obvious distortion of the news that put the law enforcer in poor light.

Later in the day, the same instructor turned on a tape recording of a mock riot. It was a role play in which some officers played the part of officers assigned to the riot. By the end of the "riot," the riot control men were barking back at the reporters, who incessantly interfered with their attempts to restore "order." The effect seemed not to be lost on the recruit class. During a break, a recruit asked me, "Don't you think [the Chicago police] were raped by the press?" The recruit class was exasperated that newsmen never seemed to take pictures showing incidents before police reactions, and never explained why an officer had his riot stick drawn back before he struck. An officer could demonstrate great restraint in the face of adversity, but the minute his arm swung upward, only then did a newsman come up with his camera. One effect, apparently lost to the recruit class, was that the "reporters" were doing what reporters are supposed to do—get information. They were simply doing their job, just as the "riot control men" were doing theirs.

The classroom was not the only place from which warnings came. Field Week gave the recruit an opportunity to hear more stories from the patrolmen on the beat. In my case, I heard two references to the press, both of them critical. Since I was assigned to one of the better precincts, the officer with whom I was on patrol brought me to one of the high-crime precincts for a short while. After I was introduced to one of the men in the precinct, he told me that just a few minutes ago he had had to mace a man. "He put one of our men in the hospital, but you won't read that in the press tomorrow," he closed.

Another officer related an attempt by the press to deliberately distort the news in order to discredit a young policeman. (I might add that I believe this officer to be of unusual high calibre in the field.)

There was this young kid who hadn't been on the outside much; he was on desk jobs all the time. One night a car sideswiped him. He followed it, got out, and identified himself as a police officer. They grabbed his nightstick and beat the hell out of him, so he drew his gun and killed one of them and shot the other. He didn't drink much, so the paper hinted he may have been coming back from a party or stopped for a drink which could have been too much for a person who didn't drink much. That's what we're up against, Rich.

As a consequence of the apparent unsympathetic treatment by reporters, who just seemed to wait for the moment an officer made a mistake, self-defense procedures, riot control, and even nightstick use were designed to display as little commotion as possible and to remain as unobvious as possible. For example, in the case of riot batons—or nightsticks, the recruit was trained to use them without ever raising them above his head. The reason specifically was to avoid giving newsmen a chance to snap a picture of an RCPD officer with his baton raised. "Keep the stick low. Just for looks." Interestingly, no mention was made that a low baton was more effective. It would be harder for it to be wrenched away, and it would be nearer to soft parts of the body.

FEMALES. Females presented the policeman with a whole new set of rules when it came to enforcing the law. Female arrests could put the officer in a very precarious situation, since women enjoyed certain sympathies not generally available to male offenders. For instance, it would be hard to explain to a passerby (who might feel his masculinity required him to "save a damsel in distress") just why an officer was struggling with a woman in a rough manner or why his hands happened to be in objectionable places.

One instructor cautioned the recruit against unnecessary female arrests. Moreover, the recruit was advised in the case of a female arrest, whether it was a juvenile or an adult, to always call his location right away, give the route of travel that he planned to take to have her booked, and possibly to call for another unit to have a witness in the car during the trip. If he did not follow these precautions, he was leaving himself open to wild accusations from the arrested party; if these precautions were followed, the courts would be more likely not to believe the complaints.

The recruit seemed to realize his particular vulnerability if a girl should scream rape or purposely tear her blouse in the course of an arrest. He traded stories about women who carried razors that they did not hesitate to use on arresting officers. He appeared to be frustrated by his apparent helplessness vis-à-vis females when he would try to conscientiously enforce the law. Several recruits asked an instructor just what they were to do if they had to search a woman.

I: Don't search a woman. Now if you're alone, remember, it's only
    her word against yours. I mean it. But they are the worst
    arrests. I've stripped some women near naked, but I've also
    seen them cut a man something fierce. Call a sergeant
    or call a matron.

R₁: What is the procedure with a female when you catch her?

I: I'd use my head and let her take the lead. I'd say, "Hi, what are you doing here with those burglary tools?" I'd check her hands and wrists; if she went to her pocket, I'd check her pocket.

R₁: But can't you 'cuff her? She's automatically wrong.

I: Are you from Rurban County? (Laughter) Well, you have it backwards—you are always in the wrong.

R₂: What if she tries a con job and rips her blouse?

I: If you think it necessary, 'cuff her. But if she's 'cuffed, she better not yell rape.

THE PUBLIC. In addition to specific groups, the general public seemed to be perceived as a "grand out-group." Although a recruit's perception of the public appeared to vary with respect to the problem at hand, it seemed that anyone who was not a law enforcer was not to be trusted. The deceit to which an officer was exposed seemed to contribute a great deal to the cynicism developed by the officer and to his perceived need to stick together with fellow officers.[17] It was difficult to adjust to the fact that those for whom he must often put his life on the line seemed to be antagonistic toward him. One instructor put it this way:

Ten years ago the policeman was a friend of the community. Not any more. You can divide any group in any manner, shape, or form, and they will have a gripe against the police.

The recruit was told never to depend too much on the public because "Joe Citizen will never give you a hand." For instance, Chicago was the real test for public support: "Sure there were mistakes made, but where were they when they could be counted?" Too many times a "victim" turned out to be the provocator; too many times an officer was duped by a person's story. In an effort to prepare the recruit for what he would encounter in the field, the instructors related some ways in which the citizen could and did take advantage of an unsuspecting policeman. During a class evaluation of Field Week, an instructor warned:

Be aware that you may be set up and accused. Never enter an

---

[17] Arthur Niederhoffer, *Behind the Shield* presents an insightful study of police cynicism. See also, Howard S. Becker and Blanche Geer, "The Fate of Idealism in Medical School," *American Sociological Review*, 23 (February 1958), pp. 50–56.

open door alone. There is the problem of the store owner claiming that some items are missing, that they were taken by the officer. I can't emphasize this enough. Don't think they won't do it. If you call on a burglary, get an assist so you have a witness . . . even though it's only one word against the other, but the inference is made, and you have to live with it.

Once again Field Week offered the recruit additional insights as to just how vulnerable he was to citizen complaints. One night the officer, with whom I was on patrol, stopped a driver in his mid-fifties who was slowly following a young girl and trying to persuade her to let him drive her to wherever she was going. We told him to pull over to the curb and parked our car in front of his. My partner walked up to the men who remained in his car.

Driver: What did I do, officer? I was just trying to be a good citizen. I'm on jury duty.

Officer: (firmly) It's very bad policy to pick up young girls, sir. Very bad policy.

He checked the driver's license and registration, and then we drove away. At the end of the tour of duty, we were called into the lieutenant's office, who was the ranking officer for the night shift. The driver had lodged a complaint, on the insistence of his sister with whom he lived, that he had been stopped and harassed for no reason at all. I was asked by the police officer to verify his story to the lieutenant.

This kind of treatment, where the officer is put in a position of constantly protecting himself from those he is supposed to be protecting, is illustrated by Wilson. He relates a story about two men who were arrested for ignoring police requests to move their car which was blocking traffic. Some force was used in the course of the arrest, and the two men were handcuffed. Onlookers protested the police action and accused the officers of brutality. Some women went so far as to beat the officers with their handbags. " 'Who's brutal to who?' a police officer later commented, bitterly."[18]

SUMMARY. Six of the eight out-groups have been discussed in terms of how they were presented and reacted to by the recruit. Significantly,

[18] James Q. Wilson, p. 226.

the definitions of the recruit and his instructors seemed to be based on the degree of control each group actually or potentially could wield over them. Each group restricted the sphere of activity of the police in some way. Where there was no direct control (as in the case of the students), the out-group in question at least seemed to have the implicit support of one or more of the other out-groups. If the recruit should ever have contact with members of any of these out-groups, he had to be wary how he interacted with them. If there was a contradiction of stories between an officer and an out-group member, the recruit believed that the officer would never be given the benefit of the doubt by the public or by his own department. Consequently, he seemed to become even more hostile to these out-groups, and more likely to devalue public opinion and to reject any attempt at extradepartmental regulation.[19]

INVISIBLE EYES

The recruit got the impression from his instruction that during patrol he had to be continuously cautious and vigilant against all out-groups. He was warned to dim his flashlight when he entered a building so he would not be noticed by a thief, and that if he had to enter a building, it was wise to have another officer with him as a witness. If he crossed an alley, he should do so carefully with his gun hand ready. However, the suspicion and vigilance with which he performed his job appeared to be projected to others. Not only was he watchful of others, he was himself being watched. This feeling of being watched by someone who could not be seen was learned in the academy and seemed to affect the recruit's orientation toward police work.

Even the criminal could be "invisible," for the officer had no clear way of distinguishing between the criminal and noncriminal as he passed them on the beat. He was told that being visible himself, he served as a crime deterrent; but he never saw those whom he was supposed to be deterring. "He may walk right past you," remarked one instructor. Because the "enemy" was invisible and because the officer learned through sad experience that out-groups and department organizations were not to be trusted, he seemed to imagine that the criminal was

---

[19] James Q. Wilson, "Police Morale, Reform, and Citizen Respect: The Chicago Case," in *The Police,* edited by David J. Bordua (New York: John Wiley, 1967), pp. 137–162.

always watching him, just waiting for a mistake that would permit the commission of a crime.

One particular recruit was concerned about an unsuspecting patrolman who might walk up to the two men involved in a murder committed the previous day, which the recruit class had been asked to help investigate.[20]

> Now that they have killed someone, they're really going to be
> desperate; now they are going to fight if they are caught. I feel
> sorry for the patrolman who doesn't know what he's getting into
> if he approaches them.

The "invisible enemy" was not just the criminal; it included the citizen. The officer must watch his behavior because there was always a chance someone would be watching him. The recruit was instructed not to stop the cars with the pretty girls all the time, because no matter "how hard you try to conceal it, someone will see you and talk about it." He was told particularly when entering a bar to report it to the desk sergeant at his next call. Otherwise, someone who noticed him enter and stay for several minutes would "start wagging his tongue."

Feelings of persecution heightened when some instructors warned the recruit about his friends outside of the department. Early in the first week, an instructor offered the advice that police information should not be shared with friends. Once a person became a policeman, "you never know who is your friend or not." The recruit conversations also reflected concern about which friends might cause the officer trouble.

> I was sitting home one night when a friend comes running in and
> yells at me, "There's a cop getting the shit knocked out of him!"
> Well, I fell for it—hook, line, and sinker. I ran out of there really
> intending to help. Out front were four guys. I asked, "Where is he,
> where's the cop who's getting beat up?" They raised their fists
> and said, "Right here!"

> I get those guys at the gas station bracing against the wall
> everytime I come by. I feel like filling a spray can with black dye
> and really put the scare on them. One time I came down with my
> shotgun, pointed in the air, and they ran out with their hands up.
> A cop was in a car across the street, he whipped up, and they

---

[20] Ernest Hemingway, "The Dangerous Summer," *Life* (Sept. 5, 1960), pp. 76–86, offers an example of an occupation in which the member deliberately increases his risk of death or injury.

cried, "We're just fooling, we're just fooling!" I told them they
could have gotten me killed. What if he came out with his gun?
Boy, was he mad. There was no reason not to think it was the
real thing.

The department, too, was watching the police officer. The recruit
was reminded of Inspection, which investigated complaints against
police officers and which was responsible for seeing that departmental standards of behavior and equipment were maintained. The
recruit was told to print out his field reports in case they were sent to
Inspection because "you don't want Inspection on your tail." If a
recruit entertained the idea of accepting a bribe from a traffic violator,
an instructor posed the question: what if the "violator" happened to
be from Inspection, making spot checks on police integrity?

Detective surveillances (stakeouts) were another source of worry
for the recruit if they were done without his knowledge. A reason
offered by several recruits for allowing an officer to know about stakeouts on his beat was that a raid would make the officer look foolish
if he were not aware of any criminal activity taking place. One
instructor tried to present a proper perspective by mentioning that the
person he liked best when he was a patrolman was the biggest book-
maker in the area. As the following statement shows, however, the
threat to the patrolman went beyond his temporary embarrassment.[21]

It is the responsibility of all officers to report all information on
vice, gambling, and narcotics sent to the Chief of Detectives.
Never be afraid that you will interfere with us. *Get it off your
chest and report it* [My emphasis]. In ———City and ———City
there have been pictures of uniformed police walking by bookies
doing their business.

Not only did the officer have to worry about someone witnessing an
error at the time of commission or omission, he also had to worry
about future consequences.

Don't erase a document. What are you trying to hide? You may
not have anything to hide, but you try telling that to a defense
attorney. . . . erring notes have a way of haunting you when you
least expect it.

The police officer did not know who might be watching him either

[21] See Erving Goffman, "Embarrassment and Social Organization," *Interaction Ritual*,
pp. 97–112, for an analysis of the relationship between embarrassment, self-image, and
social organization.

by accident or design. He must protect himself at all times. Don't stop just the pretty females; report whenever entering a bar; don't smoke on duty; don't try to overlook criminal activities—someone will always be watching at that precise moment. Even courtesy was important, not necessarily because it was the correct demeanor, but because "you don't know who you're talking to." The attitude apparently fostered by these warnings of unknown observers created and supported his feeling of persecution. If an officer should become lax or deviate intentionally from the "Rules and Procedures," someone was bound to report it. But notice, also, the precarious situation in which the department placed him.

> Criminals are a good source of information. So you cultivate
> information from honest people and dishonest people, so be aware
> of what can happen if you are indiscrete. If the purpose of your
> visitation is the cultivation of police information, then talk to him.
> Just report it . . . Fellows, it's not a question of big brother
> watching you, but God forbid, *what if he is watching*?
> [My emphasis]

MODES OF ADAPTATION

The recruit seemed to become sensitized to individual and collective protective mechanisms that operated on the field level. These mechanisms would protect him from the community and the departmental hierarchy while, in turn, he would support the hierarchy as a buffer between himself and the community. One means has already been mentioned: the establishment of formal groups that represented him to the community (through lobbies) and to the department (as bargaining agents). The Police Brotherhood Association, Detectives Association, Police Conference, and Police Association were four such groups. Still, an officer could not depend entirely on his formal group associations or "the book" in all circumstances. He had to resort to more immediate or practical protective devices. These devices were: play acting, being secretive, bending the law, and remaining emotionally uninvolved.

Before these protective mechanisms are discussed, however, another type of adaptation will be considered. Earlier it was stated that the topics of informal recruit conversations provided insights that might lead to a better understanding of police attitudes and behavior. One of the topics, monetary issues, seemed to reflect the recruit's adaptation to the requirements of the academy, the department, and life. Although it is not a protective mechanism in the same sense as the other modes, it indicates a posture toward life that, as will be shown, demands a defensive aggressiveness.

CUTTING CORNERS

The discussions of monetary issues by the recruits may be placed within a larger context that can be referred to as the "ethic of cutting corners." Cutting corners was an ethic because not only was it permissible to cut corners, it was the thing to do.

The ethic of cutting corners refers to the manipulations that attain goals with the least expenditure of effort or cost. The use of the ethic may include working the system, that is, a situation in which one uses his position in an organization for personal gain. The carpenter who keeps unused material for himself but charges his client for it just the same is working the system. Heinrich Heine worked the religious system on his deathbed when a priest mentioned that with hope God might mercifully forgive him his sins. Heine replied, "Of course he'll forgive me—that's his job." In effect, Heine was saying, "God will forgive me because I would not have anything to do with him if he did not; that is why I believe in him in the first place." Cutting corners also includes the bypassing of inconvenient rules and regulations. The police officer who bypasses due process (procedural law) to enforce substantive law, and the Department of Defense which withholds information from senators to further its own ends are examples of this aspect.

In the academy, the recruit compared the cost of his home and his land taxes with those of the other recruits. He discussed the pro's and con's of moving to one locality rather than another. He compared pay scales with the recruits from other police agencies who were also attending the academy and, if there was a difference, it resulted in some good-natured rivalry between them. If a recruit mentioned a part-time job that he had held in the past or expected to hold after he graduated from the academy, other recruits inquired into the financial rewards. When a recruit showed concern over his heating and telephone bills, recruits suggested alternative plans to help save money. When a recruit proudly explained how he was able to run his car "on a shoestring" for considerable distances, others offered further suggestions from their own expertise with cars.

Since each recruit had had experience in some other job before joining RCPD, his skills were called on or volunteered; usually they were volunteered. For instance, an ex-mason helped a recruit lay a patio in his backyard while the other repaired television sets or set up better reception systems. Another recruit did some carpentry work for a fellow recruit who lived near-by. Still another recruit offered ways to save money when buying a new car or lawn mower.

The recruit not only learned how to cut corners outside of the academy, he also learned how to cut corners within the academy. Most recruits took as few lecture notes as possible, and only as much as necessary for a passing grade when the staff inspected their note-books. Some had their wives cut their hair. Otherwise they would have had to go to a barber at least every other week in order to pass daily inspection. One recruit "cheated" when he filled out his memo book. To get him into the habit of filling out the memo book on a daily basis, each recruit was required to write down the weather conditions of each day, the times when each class began and ended, and the class subject. To avoid the inconvenience of continually pulling out his memo book anywhere from 10 to 20 times a day, this recruit filled out the day's events during the previous night.

Some ways in which academy requirements were met were in-genious. Instead of working hard to attain and maintain the glossy appearance of shoes and leather equipment, other devices were used. Some recruits used nail polish on their leather; others used the lacquer used by Polaroid for black-and-white pictures. By far the most popular item was one which, if applied properly, would require a mere wiping of the leather with a damp cloth to retain the spit-shine appearance.

Joining the police force may also be perceived as a way of cutting corners in one's life (not in the sense of cutting it short, although that, too, is involved in a dangerous occupation such as police work). If the recruit successfully passed probation, he had only 19 more years until he could retire at half pay. He could obtain high life insurance for low premiums, and he had better medical and dental care than he previ-ously could afford. According to the interviews with police investi-gators when application was made to join RCPD, 68 percent of the responses included these factors as primary reasons for joining.

There were other advantages to selecting police work as a career. The recruit fully expected to acquire various products and services at reduced prices. The use of the uniform or the shield in this way was referred to as getting something "on the arm." Some people gladly offered privileges to a police officer. For example, movie theater man-agers believed it was a good investment to permit police officers to enter for free in case of any rowdy patrons. Nevertheless, the good will of citizens was actively sought by some recruits. One recruit in particular told me that he had worn his uniform to a repair shop in the hope that his bill would be reduced. Another recruit used his "tin" following a severe snowstorm.

> I cleared my driveway several times, but each time a plow went by, it pushed the snow back up the driveway. By the third time, I got fed up and flashed my badge. I says, "Look, I've cleared this driveway three times, and each time you fill it up. How am I going to get to the station [pretending to be a full-fledged officer] if this keeps up?" He says, "Gee, if I'd known you was a cop, I would have even cleared it out for you. I'll pass the word around."

All these examples are nothing out of the ordinary. The same advice and help occur in social and religious clubs, in businesses, and between members of the same ethnic group. Indeed, entire organizations are specifically organized to obtain services at reduced rates for their members (such as travel clubs) or to obtain the greatest output for the least input (such as business enterprises). Cutting corners seems to be common to all occupations—clean or dirty. Most people try to cut costs and labor during work and leisure.

For example, Robert Merton's discussion of the bureaucratic personality indicates that although bureaucracies were structured along rational lines to increase efficiency, staff and workers eventually subverted this goal.[22] Instead of defining organizational rules as means toward the organization's goals, they defined the rules as ends in themselves. The temerity and conservatism of the typical bureaucrat is a psychological cutting of corners. That is, he is unwilling to perceive the ambivalence of issues or to think of alternative lines of action. By rigidly following the rules and by pigeonholing clients without regard for individual circumstances, the bureaucrat does not need to expend as much energy, to involve himself in the client's problem, or to take the risk of making the wrong decision as he would if he were less rigid. The police officer who views the law as an end in itself rather than as a means to justice is, in this sense, a bureaucrat and is, in this sense, cutting corners.

Is there, then, any difference between the police officer, who does dirty work, and the more respectable clean worker? Quite probably

---

[22] Robert K. Merton, "The Bureaucratic Structure and Personality," *Social Theory and Social Structure*, rev. ed. (New York: The Free Press of Glencoe, 1957), pp. 195–206.

the ethic of cutting corners is more salient in the dirty worker because he realizes that his work is, in his words, "shit work." The dirty worker may believe that, since "the system" uses him, he can get some satisfaction by using it in turn. For instance, police officers may take a second job, but it seems to be on police time that they try to catch up on their sleep.

Thus the basic difference between the cutting of corners by dirty workers and respectables is not that one is more moral, more altruistic, or more economic than the other. Instead, the basic difference seems to be that the dirty worker cuts corners in part to seek revenge against the system. If the system is going to exploit him, then he will get even by exploiting it. The businessman who cuts corners by price-fixing or the bureaucrat who cuts corners by servicing himself instead of the client is probably not out to get even with anybody or anything. His cutting of corners is a fact of life, and there is relatively little risk of punishment if a little too much of a corner is cut. The dirty worker, in contrast, is "defending by offending." He and the respectable both cut corners, but he is probably angrier when he does it, whether he acknowledges it or not.

PLAY ACTING

Play acting is the protective mechanism in which an officer pretends to play a particular role for the sake of the public. Early in the session, for instance, a recruit asked a lecturer what he should do if someone demanded that a traffic violation be enforced which the officer had not witnessed himself, or if the vehicle was no longer around when he went to the scene of the violation with the complainant. The instructor suggested that he put on a little act for the complainant's benefit. He could ask the violator for his license and then pretend he is talking to someone in the call box. Or, if the vehicle is gone, he can still go to the call box and pretend that he is following through on the complaint.

If an officer is called to the scene of an auto accident and nothing can be done for the victims, it is sometimes expedient for the officer to pretend that he is caring for them if people happen to be watching.

> After analysis of the accident, use other people and see what
> they are aware of. Use them for help. This also gets them off
> your back from seeing what you are doing and what you are
> not doing.

Thus if people's attention can be put in other directions, the officer can be relatively free to use his discretion without being witnessed.

But the audience is also protected from having to see some of the grisly things that must be done. For example, Vanderlyn R. Pine notes that following an air crash, the only reasonable way to identify victims was by their fingerprints. To get the prints, fingers were sliced off with clippers.[23]

Some of the recruits were aware of the possible risks if they did *not* play act.

R₁: You know, I got a call for my resuscitator. I never was taught how to use it, but I turned the corner on two wheels, skidded up to the house, jumped out and popped the trunk, and brought out the resuscitator. He was already dead, but the guy came up to me, "I'm glad they called you; you really know what you're doing." And I never knew what to do!

R₂: Sure, it's a big con job. You go in, you see that he's pissed and crapped in his pants. You know he's dead, but you kneel in the piss and put the resuscitator on "one." It makes a lot of impressive noise.

R₃: Shit, you go in and tell them he's dead.

R₄: You don't just walk up to the guy and say he's dead. You start giving him mouth-to-mouth resuscitation.

R₃: We never did that in Megopolis City.

R₂: The city, the city. You're out here now.

R₃: They're dead, that's all there is to it.

R₁, R₂: You aren't a doctor. You have to take care of them until they're pronounced dead. How can you tell if he's dead or not?

R₃: An ambulance man can say he's dead. What kind of training has he had?

R₁, R₂: You can't pronounce him dead, or you'll wind up behind bars for the rest of your life.

Other occupations, too, use phony techniques to cover up their own

---

[23] Vanderlyn R. Pine, "Grief Work and Dirty Work: The Aftermath of an Aircrash," *Eastern Sociological Society*, April 18, 1970.

inadequacies and lack of knowledge. The problem of the policeman seems to be that frequently his inadequacies happen to be more visible.

The department hierarchy was not above play acting either. A woman used to call a precinct regularly and complain that she had never seen a police car patrol her street since the town had joined the county police department. Finally, the desk sergeant told her to write in her complaint, which she promptly did. After a few inquiries, it was found that she was an eccentric. A polite letter was sent to her that stated that RCPD was patrolling her area in unmarked cars to better protect her. If she would stay by her window, she could spot them. A day later she called up the precinct and thanked the officers for their concern, for she had indeed stood by her window and had spotted over 20 unmarked cars!

SECRECY

The need to feel supported by the department and by his fellow officers seemed to be an important component of the patrolman's working personality if he were to confidently fulfill his functions. If they would not support him in small matters, how could he expect them to come to his aid in a difficult or dangerous situation? The occupational need for having colleagues with a strong sense of solidarity seemed to contribute to the officer's distrust of outsiders, who more likely than not could not be counted on when they were most needed. The feeling of distrust of outsiders, the strong sense of togetherness among themselves, and the need to defend their actions from public or departmental inquiries seemed to contribute to the development of a norm of secrecy among police officers.

Several times instructors requested the recruit not to discuss some of the things that he had learned in class with anyone outside the department.

> This is confidential what we're telling you here. Don't go
> blabbing it around because all you'll do is tell somebody how
> to do it who doesn't know it yet. . . . Make them work for their
> information.

These warnings, coupled with the definitions of out-groups, including the recruit's friends, seemed to contribute to the norm of secrecy so strongly that an officer who witnessed another officer's illegal activities might not be quick to report it, if he decided to report it at all. One study suggested that officers might even be willing to perjure themselves to protect a fellow officer.[24] Whether the norm of secrecy was that cogent in RCPD is questionable, but it seemed strong enough to unify the patrolmen in order to keep indiscretions from the knowledge of superiors, Inspection, or the community. For example, I spoke to a patrolman who had broken a couple of serious regulations but whose fellow officers covered up for him. Since professionals are accorded the right to judge their own members, the maintenance of secrecy was one motivating factor in the patrolmen's attempt to extend the label of profession to police work. This point is elaborated on in the next chapter, "Professionalization."

LEGAL DEVIATIONS

The defensiveness of the recruit also had its effect on his perception of law enforcement. Taught to be constantly alert to the unexpected and to the many ways in which he could endanger himself or his career, the recruit seemed to subordinate due process of law, substantive law, and the department's rules and regulations to his personal safety. For instance, when the recruits were asked what they would do if someone grabbed their mace in a struggle, they responded collectively, "Shoot 'em!" The staff, apparently shocked by their response, offered several alternative lines of action that they could take. To the recruits, however, there was only one reasonable response, regardless of its legal ramifications: the one that guaranteed their physical safety. This perspective was legitimated by an instructor and later by an FBI agent.

> The only reason you have a gun is to protect yourself. No one likes to kill a fourteen year old kid . . . You may not know at the time he is a kid, so watch it. If you think he's going for a knife or gun, shoot. I'd rather go to a grand jury than to a funeral, that's for sure.

> I'd rather use unnecessary force than have someone tell my widow I was afraid of his civil rights.

---

[24] William A. Westley, "Secrecy and the Police." However, in *An Examination of Role Theory: The Case of the State Police* (Lincoln: The University of Nebraska Press, 1966), pp. 101–104, Jack J. Preiss and Howard J. Ehrlich dispute Westley's importance of the norm of secrecy. They claim that 61 percent of officers in their sample would report fellow officers *if* the consequences of rule breaking would affect the public, the department, or fellow officers.

Here, then, is another dirty aspect of police work. If an officer shoots or kills a youth, the public becomes indignant. Yet, the youth could have been about to kill the officer; a 14-year-old boy has no difficulty in pulling a trigger. To the officer, the public response means that they would rather see the officer killed instead.

In some instances, self-protection meant breaking the law. For example, the state law permitted the officer to search a person for weapons only on "probable suspicion" (when he knew a crime had been committed in the area, or the person looked like the suspect described over the car radio, or the officer believed himself to be in danger), not by hunches. If the officer drew his gun before a person did anything out of the ordinary—before he was in "reasonable danger of life or limb"—he was breaking the state law. The recruit seemed to have no compunctions about doing just that if he thought it necessary. One said:

> When you go into an alley, according to the "stop and frisk"
> law, you are supposed to talk to him first. Then out of that you
> either let him go, arrest him, or see if he has anything to frisk
> him on. Actually you can give almost any excuse or think of
> an acceptable one and get away with it. You have to do it,
> or you'll be dead.

The recruit's tendency to deviate from the law was evident during an evening of role playing. In each role-play situation, the recruit chose from among alternative lines of action the option that *he* thought to be safest for himself. The end result, however, was that the "safest" option actually engendered more danger to him.[25] In one scene, for example, a recruit was told that he was on patrol, and he would come across several whites fighting a lone black in an all-white neighborhood. What he was not told was that the whites started the fight. As the recruit selected for the role play discovered the fight, the black was defending himself with a pipe which he had picked up from the "street." The recruit came up from behind the black, struggled with him, and grabbed the pipe from the black's hands. Then he went over to the whites for an explanation. Because the black kept interrupting to present his side of the story, the recruit handcuffed him to keep him quiet.

---

[25] See Albert P. Cardarelli, "An Analysis of Police Killed by Criminal Action," *Journal of Criminal Law, Criminology, and Police Science*, 59 (September 1968), pp. 447–453; Ronald Tauber, "Danger and the Police: A Theoretical Analysis," *Issues in Criminology*, 3 (1967), pp. 69–81; and Arthur E. Hippler, pp. 56–63.

At the evaluation period following the role-playing scene, the staff and recruits discussed the incident. The recruits were told that it would have been more strategic not to have charged into the fracas to grab the pipe away from the black, because the black had no way of knowing that the person coming from behind him was a "policeman." The recruits disagreed: first and foremost was the need to disarm the black in case he decided *not* to obey the officer's command.

The same role play pointed to another ambiguous point that contributed to the recruit's hesitancy to enforce the law as he saw it. During the scene, the black was handcuffed. Early in the training period, the recruit learned that the minute he put handcuffs on a suspect or stopped him from going where he wanted, the person was under arrest even though no words to that effect were used. Since the black was under de facto arrest, could the officer be sued for false arrest? As far as the recruit was concerned, no explanation by the instructors seemed satisfying enough to allay his worry.

UNINVOLVEMENT

The purpose of the foregoing has been to demonstrate how the recruit acquires a defensive ethos even before he leaves the police academy. If the recruit does not act defensively and rigidly once he becomes a patrolman, how else should he act? How else *can* he act? Although the police officer's duty is to regulate the behavior of the members of his community, in a democratic society it becomes necessary to regulate the regulators. For what many policemen choose to overlook is that their relationship with a citizen is unlike any other kind of relationship. If a citizen decides not to show the officer respect or if he chooses to leave the encounter, the officer can use force to continue the interaction with the threat of violence or arrest.

In response to community suspicions, the higher echelons attempt to regulate the behavior of their subordinates to reduce incipient antagonism as much as possible. Consequently, the department as a whole finds itself fighting on two fronts while trying to maintain law and order. On one front it must convince the community that police work is necessary and that it is performing its tasks as well as can be expected. The means by which the department tries to convince the community of this include crime statistics, clearance rates, field reports, a bureau of community relations, and internal policing.

On the other front the department has to control the behavior of its subordinate members, particularly the patrolmen. The department handles this difficulty through elaborate rules and procedures, a military pattern of hierarchical relationships, and by checking on independent action through a system of field reports and an inspection squad. Recognizing the patrolman's vulnerability and helplessness in the face of community pressures, the department tries to reduce the options where the officers think there are too many (for example, first aid) and to increase the options where the officers think there are too few (for example, fights in progress).

The recruit, however, seems to think that he is fighting on two fronts also. He, too, realizes he has to govern his actions so as not to arouse community criticism against himself or against the department. Yet, he finds that not only must he defend his actions to the public, he has to defend them to his superiors as well. The recruit believes that the department, instead of protecting the patrolman's right to unencumbered action and supporting him if a complaint were lodged against him, expresses its distrust of him through the mechanisms used to control—and to protect him from the consequences of—his inclination to use his own discretion.

Wilson's discussion on police discretion in law enforcement is based on the premise that police behavior is often inconsistent because of its low observability. "Because he works alone his superior can never know exactly what happened and must take either his word or the complainant's."[26] This low observability permits the officer to use a great deal of discretion. However, his observation may not be as cogent as it appears, since he ignores the phenomenological facet of police work. That is, whether or not the patrolman enjoys low observability in fact, may be relatively unimportant compared to how observable he himself thinks he is. The superior may not know the exact circumstances of a situation, but the recruit seemed to feel that his actions would become observable through complaints, editorials, Inspection investigations, and the like.

From the perspective of the recruit, the law, too, seems to present a threat to his well-being. Nevertheless, H. Taylor Buckner implies that the law is perceived as rules of the game by which police officers

---

[26] James Q. Wilson, *Varieties of Police Behavior*, p. 72.

compete for a conviction against the offender, the lawyer, the district attorney, the judge, and the jury.[27] This theme was expressed in the academy by recruit and instructor alike, but it was not very strong. Essentially, the law was presented and received as a body of rules to worry about. The discrepancy may possibly be explained by the fact that Buckner was studying men who operated in the field. Perhaps as the recruits become more knowledgeable in the law, they become confident enough to perceive law enforcement as a game with the courts. However, the instructors are brought to the academy precisely because they are men who actively work in the field. Apparently, both perspectives can operate at the field level.

The patrolman's occupation is dangerous—dangerous for himself, his family, and the people with whom he comes into contact. If he is to remain physically and economically intact, he has no choice but to suppress his creative or independent initiative in favor of following rules and obeying orders. He must protect himself from possible law suits or departmental discipline. He must be concerned about unexpected situations that may cost him his life. He must watch out for particular groups that can exert political power over him because experience demonstrates their deceit. He must learn to protect himself from all angles in case "someone" is watching him who is ready to report innocent blunders or deliberate peccadillos. Not only has he a need to protect himself from out-groups but also he must be alert to certain elements within his own group. For instance, Niederhoffer observes in his study that patrolmen have a "morbid fear that someone will write a letter of complaint to the commissioner" about them.[28] Furthermore, he is in an organization in which there are few positive guides for action and many rules to remember, making it rather easy to be penalized if a superior officer has the inclination.

Under these organizational and interpersonal strains, the reactions of the recruit appear to be quite natural. Secrecy is necessary because the many rules and regulations cannot be adhered to completely. Certainly it would be foolish to admit mistakes to suspicious and hostile out-groups. Playacting is one means of covering up his inadequacies in front of his clientele. However, the unhealthy component

---

[27] H. Taylor Buckner, "The Police: The Culture of a Social Control Agency" (unpublished Ph.D. dissertation), University of California at Berkeley, 1967.
[28] Arthur Niederhoffer, p. 109.

of secrecy is the refusal of police officers to acknowledge the truth (if it were to involve criticism of them) to outsiders, although they very probably acknowledge it among themselves. As one RCPD patrolman complained, "We have to protect ourselves, nobody else will." But from the standpoint of police critics, any cover-ups by police officers provide further evidence that policemen are not to be trusted and confirm the legitimacy of their distrust. The frustrations arising from his apparent powerlessness to enforce the law convinces the recruit that, if he were to enforce the law at all, he must circumvent procedural rules of law.

Still another response is to resort to "deadly physical force" (firearms) as a *first* line of defense rather than as the last alternative, since it seems to be the safest option for the young officer. But the use of deadly physical force may back an opponent into a corner to the point where he may think his only recourse is to use deadly physical force himself. What is thought to be most protective turns out to increase the danger to the officer. Of course, part of the motivation to handle situations without backing down or calling the precinct for help is what he thinks his fellow officers will think of him if he cannot handle the situation himself. But the end result still tends to put him in further jeopardy.

In spite of all that the recruit learns in the academy, he is still expected to perform his duties confidently, boldly, and wisely. The staff and some of the instructors try to explain that mistakes will be made, but that an officer need not worry if he performs his job with honest intentions. "Remember," he is told, "the only guy who doesn't make mistakes doesn't do anything." Before the recruit left the academy for his one week of field training, a staff member stated, "The boss says, 'If you make mistakes, I know you're working.' And I know he'll back you to the hilt." The recruit was told he might even have to break the rules at times.

> This means if there is an emergency, do what is necessary and
> break the rules. You've got to have the balls to do what you
> feel is right. Do it, even if you get chewed out a little.

These items of encouragement cannot undo all the other warnings. The recruit has to be warned about possible dangers, but the effect is to produce a recruit who is security conscious. To be told it is "*not* doing your job that gets you in trouble" does not bolster the recruit's confidence. He has learned that there are too many ways to go wrong, and he is not about to gamble away a secure civil service job with good pay, early retirement, and a high pension after only 20 years of work.[29] The immediate goal of the recruit is to successfully pass his one year's probation. Penalties await the officer who tackles difficult situations or who deviates from departmental procedures. Security awaits the officer who has no complaints in his file and who sticks to the book in most situations. To actively maintain order or to enforce the law without being directed to from the precinct or headquarters can be disastrous. The recruit's frequently used phrase, "don't get involved," is more of a warning than the joking manner in which it is said seems to indicate.

Aware of its constant defensiveness toward the community (which was picked up by the recruit), the department tried to increase its range of autonomy by changing the stereotype of the police officer that appeared to be held by the community. It tried to convince both the community and its own members that this new image lay in professionalism. It is this process that we now consider.

---

[29] Compare with the casino personnel in Erving Goffman's *Where the Action Is*, p. 193; and Ian Lewis' "On the Pinnacles of Power: The Advertising Man," *The Human Shape of Work*, edited by Peter L. Berger (New York: Macmillan, 1964), pp. 113–180.

Every man of ambition has to fight his century
with its own weapons. What this century worships is
wealth. The God of this century is wealth. At all
costs one must have wealth.
Oscar Wilde, "An Ideal Husband"

Professionalization.

CHAPTER FOUR

THE PHENOMENOLOGICAL APPROACH

The precise meaning of the term "profession" has long been the subject of debate among students of occupations. On the one hand, the term has been applied to a select group of occupations such as law, medicine, and theology. Taking these occupations as models, students have abstracted qualities that can serve as criteria to determine whether or not an occupation is a profession. On the other hand, so many occupational groups claim the status of profession that the term is virtually meaningless—except to the occupational members themselves. Morticians, realtors, nurses, engineering technicians, journalists, librarians, druggists, and chiropractors are some of the occupations that have entered or are trying to enter the professional ranks. With such a state of affairs, some students have argued that the definition of profession is limited, since it implies that each criterion must be satisfied if an occupation is to qualify. Howard Becker evades the definitional problem by suggesting that if a group succeeds in getting itself called a profession, then for all practical purposes it is a profession.[1]

Everett C. Hughes, however, offers a different framework entirely. He believes that a description of characteristics of a profession to which aspiring occupations may be compared in their own effort to become "professional" should be a secondary focus in occupational

---

[1] Howard S. Becker, "The Nature of a Profession," *Education for the Professions*, 61st Yearbook of the Society for the Study of Education, Part 2 (Chicago: University of Chicago Press, 1962), p. 33.

research. Such studies neglect the phenomenological facet of professionalism: that is, how do the occupational members themselves define a profession or professional? In the phenomenological orientation, the objective standards, which in essence define what a profession is, become meaningless apart from what the term means to the occupational members. Hughes advises researchers to refrain from continually asking the secondary question: Is this occupation a profession? The circumstances and steps that members of an occupation take to attain the status of profession are more fundamental issues for investigation than is guessing at traits that make up an "objective" definition of profession. The term "profession" is *primarily* subjective, connoting value and prestige to the occupational members and to those outside the occupation.[2]

This is not to say that Hughes was not concerned about the characteristics of so-called professions, since he pointed out some characteristics of his own.[3] A professionally striving group claims that its work is a matter of broad public concern which involves privilege to information on matters of life and death, and honor and dishonor. Since the client is not in a position to judge the quality of the service he receives, the group contends that only a colleague group has the right to make a judgment about whether or not a mistake was made by a member of the colleague group. In an attempt to maintain the guise of competence by keeping internal disagreements unobservable to those not in the colleague group, the group establishes a licensing system that is sanctioned by the state. The licensing system allows the group to make its own standards of admission and to discipline colleagues as it sees fit. Nevertheless, the objective state of affairs is not a paramount question. How the members define the situation and attempt to convince others of their rightful place in the hierarchy is.

While researchers admit that the process of professionalization is an important facet of study, in actual practice research in the subjective tradition remains sparse compared to research in the objective tradition. Students of occupations casually dismiss the Hughesian approach and seem to place more confidence in the objective perspective. Certainly this appears to be the case in the literature regarding the police: profession and professionalism are used as if they

[2] Everett C. Hughes, "Professions," *Professions in America*, edited by Kenneth S. Lynn and *Daedalus* (Boston: Beacon Press, 1965), pp. 242–260; and *Men and Their Work* (Chicago: Free Press, 1958), pp. 44–45.
[3] Everett C. Hughes, *Men and Their Work*, pp. 94–95, 116–117, and 140–143.

described objective criteria. Scholars and police officials alike explain in what ways policemen are, or are not, professionals or are, or are not, craftsmen. Police officers claim that they are professional; scholars conclude that police are more like craftsmen. To elaborate this point, I refer to two recent studies on the police that specifically deal with police professionalism.

Jerome Skolnick lists two main traditions in the sociological literature regarding professions.[4] One stems from Durkheim's conception of a profession that is based on an enforceable code of ethics. In addition to having high status and a monopoly over certain activities, professions are distinctive in that they infuse their work organization "with moral values, plus the use of sanctions to insure that these moral values are upheld." The second tradition stems from Weber's emphasis on technical efficiency and smoothness. Skolnick notes that police reformers speak of professionalism according to Weber's model of managerial efficiency while they neglect Durkheim's concern about a moral code of ethics. The reason for this, he explains, lies in two conflicting principles of police work: maintaining order and subscribing to the rule of due process of law. Because police efficiency is based on their clearance rates, police officers perceive themselves as controllers of misconduct through the invoking of punitive sanctions, rather than as legal actors within a democratic society. They conceive of themselves as skilled workers who should be free of external authorities, rather than as civil servants who are obliged to comply with the rule of law. The police officer's ideology is that of a craftsman, not of a professional. Although Skolnick is very perceptive in his discussion, just what the difference is between a craftsman and a professional remains unclear. The craftsman demands autonomy, but the professional does, too. The policeman may not comply with the rule of due process of law, but the doctor does not comply with the Hippocratic oath either.

Arthur Niederhoffer goes so far as to list the criteria that define a profession.[5] They are: (1) high standards of admission, (2) a special body of knowledge and theory, (3) a code of ethics, (4) altruism and dedication to a service ideal, (5) a lengthy period of training for candidates, (6) licensing of members, (7) autonomous control, (8)

[4] Jerome H. Skolnick, *Justice Without Trial* (New York: John Wiley, 1966), pp. 230–245.
[5] Arthur Niederhoffer, *Behind the Shield* (Garden City, N.Y.: Doubleday, 1967), pp. 18–19.

pride of the members in their profession, and (9) publicly recognized status and prestige. If professionalism is perceived as a continuum, the police should be well-along the road to their goal. They have a code of ethics, professional associations, service ideals, and admission and training standards. Of course, one could argue that police standards are too low to begin with, that the code of ethics is unenforceable, or that the police associations are more like unions than esoteric groups dedicated to improving the quality of their profession. But this begs the question. The point is, what are "high admission standards"? How "autonomous" must an occupation be? Is training by apprenticeship, or is it by classroom study and research? Niederhoffer believes that the New York City police are not professional because the PBA relies on demagoguery as a means of persuasion and is not altruistic.[6] The politics of the New York PBA is well-known, but the AMA has also resorted to distortion, name-calling, and demagoguery when it became the subject for reform. Yet, which occupation is less professional?

My main concern, however, is not whether police work is a profession or not. Instead, I adopt Hughes' phenomenological approach to find out what the police themselves think a professional is and how they go about convincing the public that they are professionals. Topics that I discuss include:

(1) how the professional image is defined to in-coming members,

(2) the elements of which the professional image was comprised during recruit training,

(3) the contribution of the image to a framework for judging others and oneself,

(4) the ways in which the image has organizational support or has not,

(5) the meaning the image seems to have for the recruits themselves, and

(6) how it may have influenced recruit perceptions toward law and justice as they leave for the field.

[6] Arthur Niederhoffer, pp. 175, 185–186.

FIRST STEPS TOWARD PROFESSIONALISM

EDUCATION

The same day the recruit took the oath making him a bona fide member of the department, he was given a brief introductory speech while he stood at attention on the drill floor with the other in-coming members. He was at once instructed that he was a professional within a profession and must act accordingly. "You will look like professionals, read like professionals, and study like professionals who are joining other professionals in a profession within the community." It was not until later in the day that the recruit was finally given a hint of what was meant by "professional."

Education was presented as the sine qua non, the indispensable ingredient, of professionalism. That is, the recruit was told that a professional is "recognized by his education"; if RCPD wanted to be professional, its members had to be educated. But while education might have been the key to attaining professional status, high salary seemed to be the real criterion for success. Said one instructor:

You may come up against someone who won't join law
enforcement because of the pay. And you'll be able to say,
"Whoo, we're professionals. We require a minimum of two years
of college and we can start at $15,000." Education is the thing.

During a coffee break, a recruit offered his opinion. If the community wanted professional policemen, it would have to pay for it. ". . . I can tell you why all these guys are here: for the retirement and for the security. You've gotta have the money if you want professionals."

To become acquainted with their educational opportunities, the recruit class spent a day at State College where there was a police science program. The program consisted of a two-year college level degree and covered three required areas. The number following each subject equals its semester hours.

Area 1:   Sociology 3, Psychology 3, Physical Science 6, English 6
Area 2:   Police Science courses (law, traffic) 36
Area 3:   Electives in Social Sciences and the Humanities 10

The state allowed the academy training session to be worth five semester hours, which would be applied to Area 3, in order to encourage the recruit to enter the program. In effect, the liberal arts courses were superseded by police technology courses. By not applying the five credits to Area 2 (which would seem to be the appropriate choice), the department and State College emphasized courses that were mainly technological. Instead of giving priority to courses that were more likely—but certainly no guarantee—to cultivate the use of reason, contemplation, and discourse as instruments for achieving order, "nuts and bolts" courses took precedence. RCPD and the state might have believed that education was necessary for the development of a well-rounded police officer, but unlike the professions that they try to emulate, the quality of their education was essentially vocational.

ESPRIT DE CORPS

Even with the vocational orientation in the police science curriculum, the recruit was taught that he was more professional than the members of the classical professions of medicine, law, theology, and education. The police profession became the superprofession, one that overlapped with each of the elite professions but performed its job with more dedication. A tinge of self-righteousness ran throughout a lecture presented by a popular instructor which seemed to set the tone regarding professions for the duration of the session.

> I submit, too, gentlemen, that the average attorney is not as dedicated as the average law enforcer. When you get your gun, you are given the power of life and death. Not even the Supreme Court has that power. I submit to you that the legal attorney is guilty of moral prostitution—by that I mean he says one thing and means another. The 1920's showed how an attorney who could circumvent the law was hailed as successful—one who could twist a perhaps inept police testimony.
>
> The leading attorney is not F. Lee Bailey, but Mr. Foreman, who defended Candy and her nephew, who were in an incestuous relationship (but after seeing her picture, you could forgive him that) and who conspired in killing her husband. Yet Foreman got an acquittal. And I quote from Foreman after the trial, "My clients want freedom, not justice." It's rare when a police officer bastardizes the law, while I feel attorneys do, and Foreman succinctly stated their position. The public is very willing to retain the stereotype of the fat, slouchy policeman. We're trying to change that stereotype.
>
> Now let's talk about medicine. Here again we take a profession which used to be dedicated to the citizenry turning to the cash register. One night you may have a grisly accident on Franklin Turnpike that turns your stomach, don't pick up a phone to call a doctor because you won't get one. Your first aid is what saves lives. If you and your first aid weren't there, he'd be in the

morgue. The average physician here is making $40,000 clear. A number of med schools have even dropped giving the Oath of Hippocrates. Someone must have had a conscience and realized that it didn't apply to the present medical profession.

... We are bound to get some bad apples who smear the badge; what they do smears the badge of everybody across the country. Every profession has its cancers. How many of the clergy betray the cloth by going into sex? How many educators hide behind academia—the homosexuals who warp our children's minds? At least when we get a bad apple, we get rid of him.

The disparagement of the elite professions by the lecturer apparently found willing ears among the recruits, some of whom had their own stories about lawyers and doctors. As in the lecture, the lawyer was never given the benefit of the doubt: he connives to distort the law for his own selfish ends. Tales abounded about the lawyer who got his client off through a legal technicality. As for the doctor, recruits complained how useless it was to try to get a doctor to make a house call. One recruit who had been an ambulance driver recounted an experience of his at a hospital. He had brought a badly injured car accident victim into the emergency room. Because the victim was a "mess," the attendants walked by pretending not to see him. Finally, the driver grabbed a doctor and ordered him to take care of the injured man. "That's the way you have to talk to them," he finished.

Not only was law enforcement projected as the most noble and sincere profession, but the instructors increased recruit enthusiasm and professional distinctiveness by setting up their own department as a paradigm for other police departments.

If you stay with us, we can be the best—including Metropolis Department; they aren't so good. And with all due respect to those from Megopolis Department, all they have is size and strength; but they can't compare to us because we're professional, and we want to be professional about our job.

Recruits who came from other police departments confirmed the excellence of RCPD. From the first day of the training session, these recruits compared their departments unfavorably with Rurban County's. Several recruits from Megopolis Department referred to it as "the factory." One of them told me that 55 percent of the force would "love to leave Megopolis Department, but they are either over-age or cannot afford the move." Another recruit remarked about a city policeman who gave up a soft job in order to stay on the beat. "He was really dedicated, that's very rare; out here, everyone is dedicated." Still another recruit explained, "We were told not to make any arrests. They kept trying to stop me, but I wouldn't . . . We were told right off not to make any arrests, not to get involved."

Suburban County Police Department, contiguous to Rurban County, fared no better. "They accept false rumors and get rid of you. They back you up all right—with a knife in your back." And, "Jeff even went through Suburban Academy before he came here, but he quit; he saw right away that it was political. You never know where you stand."

In summary, the first steps taken by the staff and visiting lecturers seemed to be the construction of a feeling of specialness—a "we are best" syndrome. The law enforcer was not just equal to the professional with the most status, he was better. Professions were in a hierarchical relationship to one another with law enforcement at the apex. And within the law enforcement profession itself, RCPD was the best. The lateral relationship in which a professional is recognized as an expert in his respective area seems to characterize the "classical" professions because they are secure in their status. On the other hand, the insecure occupations such as law enforcement are too insecure and too competitive to feel comfortable in a lateral relationship, especially when they have not been recognized by those who have "arrived." To be told that the recruit would learn in 12 weeks what the lawyer had to know for his bar examinations reinforced these feelings of inequity. In the following section, the content of the "professional image" as it seemed to be defined to the recruit will be examined.

THE PROFESSIONAL IMAGE

THE PHYSICAL IMAGE

Once having established an espirit de corps, it remained for the instructors to teach the recruit to be a professional police officer. One way was to look the part. Great stress was placed on the recruit's physical appearance. At first, the emphasis was not apparent.

> We aren't going to inspect you today, but we expect you to
> always have a neat appearnce. Shoes are to be shined . . .
> Haircuts are preferred to be crew cuts; we aren't strict, but we
> won't tolerate long sideburns or pompadours.

The recruit soon learned that shined shoes were not enough: they had to be spit-shined on the toe at the very least. Even the recruit's leather equipment (holster, belt, handcuff case, and bullet case) had to be as close to a spit-shine as possible. The result was a patent leather look that seemed to contradict the recruit's image of himself as an officer of the law and as a man of action. Regular haircuts were not enough either. While the staff had said crew cuts were not required, the recruit found that they might just as well have been required.

On the other hand, the staff claimed that the requirements they placed on the recruits' physical appearance were necessary because "with fifty-four recruits, we don't have time to worry about a picayune thing like appearance." Judging from the amount of time the staff spent on inspections during the training session, however, appearance had to be more than a picayune matter. Shoes not only had to be polished, they had to be spit-shined. Haircuts could not only be neat, they had to be cut almost weekly. Uniforms not only had to be tidy, they had to be ironed after each day's use.

Surely the staff had other criteria in mind by which to evaluate a recruit's appearance than what it at first described as a "neat appearance." The stress on the recruit's dress habits was more than an expression of discipline although that, too, was involved. Nor could it be explained away as part of a hazing process characteristic of fraternal or military organizations as an essential part of their rites of passage.[7] For example, a staff member wrote me about this. He thought I might have missed the point of inspections: "The minute harassment was only designed to make the new man, who would be wearing the uniform for the first time, more conscious of his appearance." On a recognized and intended level he is, of course, correct. But on an unrecognized and unintended level, the attitude that seemed to be translated to the recruit was that a neat physical appearance *was* professional.

Appearance was not only an end in itself, that is, professional, but it was also a means to convince the public that a new breed of policeman was at its service. Whereas the "old style" cop might have been sloppy, overweight, and cigar smoking—the image associated with police corruption—the image of the new breed would replace the stereotype. As one instructor put it baldly, "Look sharp and impress the public." In spite of the instructors' insistence on a new breed of

---

[7] Sanford Dornbusch, "The Military Academy as an Assimilating Institution," *Social Forces*, 33 (May 1955), pp. 316–321; Arnold Van Gennup, *Rites of Passage* (Chicago: University of Chicago Press, 1960); Frank W. Young, *Initiation Ceremonies* (New York: Bobbs-Merrill, 1965).

police officer, a few interesting incidents suggested that at times something resembling the old breed was still desirable.

The tenth day of the session, the staff selected several men from each of our two platoons. The recruits were to shout commands to their respective platoons, and the two who performed to the staff's satisfaction would become platoon sergeants. What struck me was that the recruit who became my platoon sergeant seemed to earn his position by booming Neanderthal grunts, for I never understood a command he gave. It was as if he were chosen on volume alone. Nevertheless, the "sharp appearance" and the deep voice of authority expressed a realistic need in the field. Said one instructor, "In this job if you don't look the part, forget it. You must project confidence. You are going to be put into an emergency situation sometime in your career, and you have to step in and take charge when everybody else is emotional." Thus, a large and necessary part of the emphasis on appearance seemed to be for its effect on the public.

The second incident occurred right after the completion of the first week of the session. During the night a severe snowstorm put the community into an official state of emergency. Protocol was for a recruit to call the academy 15 minutes before roll call if he would be late or absent during the day. Most recruits, including myself, had called up to find out if classes would be held that day. We were informed by Headquarters that classes were canceled. However, a few recruits had not checked about classes and had staunchly made the trip. For salary adjustments because of the cancellation, the pay for the missed day was to be applied to the day that a recruit would spend at the Communications Center during a weekend. Those recruits who had come to the academy in the aftermath of the storm and found the doors closed were to be paid in full for the day that they would spend at Communications.

The other recruits balked at the rewards granted to those who came to the academy (or at the punishment received for not coming). Their feeling was either that it was impossible to reach the academy and the matter was out of their hands, or that they would have come to the academy if classes had met. Nevertheless, it was interesting that the department rewarded those recruits who did not have the fore-sight to call headquarters before leaving their homes, while those who did not bulldog their way to the academy were penalized. It became a question of which kind of recruit the department actually wanted: the one who would charge straight ahead impervious to the conditions surrounding him (as the brave but unthinking soldier assaulting a defended hill), or the one who would respond to a situation flexibly and with deliberation (supposedly a characteristic of the new breed). The department seemed to have opted for the "heroic" style.[8]

THE MORAL IMAGE

The physical image seemed to be closely associated with the moral image, which connotes respectability, convention, piety, virtue, and honor. Physical appearance was used as an indicator of a person's place in the moral structure. A person who shaved each day, kept his hair short, shined his shoes regularly, and wore pressed clothes could be expected to be a respectable, law-abiding, and moral person. Conversely, those persons who grew beards, wore their hair long, and wore unkempt clothes—in short, those who deviated from convention —could be expected to connote something less than the moral.

> Kids want to be like adults in some ways. They want sex, but
> not the responsibilities that go with it . . . or I'll braid my hair for
> spite . . . So we want good appearances. Everything is going
> to look good.

Therefore, the recruit was told he was not allowed to grow sideburns, mustaches, or long hair because he had to "set an example" for the citizenry and because he would then offend fewer people. (I understand that the academy has since become more lax in this respect.)

Of course, there was a screening process that included an evaluation of how the investigators thought the candidate would project the new police image before he was admitted to RCPD. Only one recruit in the class had been given a decidedly unfavorable report during his precandidacy interview. His report read something like this: needed a shave, haircut, hair hanging over his ears and shirt collar [he had a "mod" haircut]; he lacked any kind of military bearing, slouching down in chair during interview; he lacked enthusiasm shown by other candidates. Although his appearance obviously did not disqualify him, and he did have an opportunity to "prove" himself, it is interesting that his hair style and mannerisms during the interview were questionable in the eyes of the interviewers. In contrast, candidates from other law enforcing agencies had the following remark of approval: he has the background that indicates he can adjust to police work well. There was no further elaboration; the fact that the

---

[8] Morris Janowitz, *The Professional Soldier* (New York: The Free Press, 1960), p. 21.

applicant had some previous police experience made him a suitable candidate. The former recruit, however, did not have the image that the department hoped to project to the public; he looked too unconventional for them. Ironically, I thought he was one of the few recruits who believed in and tried to conform to the "new image" beyond surface manifestations.

While this aspect of the moral image may be offensive to some readers, it nevertheless exists and has a bearing on police behavior. No instructor, no staff member, and no recruit ever explicitly stated that a person's physical appearance was a sign of his moral worth. But inferences can be and were made based on comments regarding the unconventionally attired. No instructor made a positive or accepting statement about the unconventionally dressed; only two recruits verbalized their tolerance for such persons. Furthermore, it seemed to be the general consensus that people with long hair or a beard, for example, deserved a different quality of law enforcement than their opposites. Here, then, is another example of a process and relationship that may not have been intended or recognized but did exist and should be recognized.

Integrity, the capacity to be honest with oneself and with others, was the second component of the moral image as it seemed to be presented to the recruit. "Without integrity you cannot be a professional." The recruit seemed to think he had this quality: that was one reason why he entered law enforcement. Consequently, he resented persons in the elite professions who did not always display moral characters, yet apparently had a monopoly of high salaries and prestige. The police officer was only trying to do his job, what the people hired him to do, but all he seemed to find were stumbling blocks in his path. The doctor, lawyer, clergyman, and educator did not seem to fulfill their jobs with as much personal sacrifice and moral discipline as the policeman did, yet the public refused to treat him as a professional. To the recruit, the disparity of rewards seemed unjust. The righteous indignation directed toward the elite professions increased his feeling of moral superiority. This feeling of superiority seemed to serve as a basis for an in-group identity that was continuously set off against the implied moral inferiority of various outgroups. In his envy of the elite professions, he deprecated them and thereby bolstered his own self-image.

THE COURTEOUS IMAGE ·
Professionalism included what a patrolman *did* as well as how he looked.

> Every person who walks in the precinct is entitled at that moment to your undivided attention—whether he is green, a Buddhist, or an atheist. We are going to expose you to the worst kind of treatment, and how you handle it will determine whether you're a professional or just another policeman.

Various reasons were given to the recruit as to why he should behave courteously. One of these reasons was defensive. That is, one should be courteous because the public generalizes from the behavior of one policeman to every policeman in the nation. The department and recruit seemed to resent this necessity for being defensive, since they considered themselves professionals of good moral character. Apparently, anybody could be discourteous to a policeman, but he in turn could not be. "But how you respond to this is what makes the difference between a professional or unprofessional." Hearing this, the recruit responded, "What about our side, don't they care about us?"

Another reason offered to the recruit for acting courteously was that the way a patrolman presented himself could aid him in performing his duties with the least amount of trouble.[9]

> Treat lovers nice. There's no reason to bust their balls. Because they don't forget it. Today we have to use professionalization. Give them time to adjust themselves if you suspect any hanky-panky.

Thus, as one's physical appearance seemed to be identified with professionalism, courtesy was also.

The community itself seemed to support politeness, self-control, and deference as definitions of professionalism. During a sit-in at State University, the police department was commended by community newspapers for its "professional" behavior. Deans, professors, and police officials kept the situation cool and persuaded most of the demonstrators to leave the building. The few students who remained were arrested and escorted out without harshness or bodily harm.

[9] Erving Goffman, "The Nature of Deference and Demeanor," *Interaction Ritual* (Chicago: Aldine, 1967), pp. 57–95, and *The Presentation of Self in Everyday Life* (Garden City, N.Y.: Doubleday, 1959), pp. 104 and 217, discuss the role of courtesy as a basis for normal face-to-face interaction.

The police department was praised for "looking good," they "looked like professionals."

The professional image, then, had three components: appearance, morality, and demeanor. Although these components were defined as ends in themselves, for the most part, the rationale for them seemed to be expediency.

THE PROFESSIONAL IMAGE AND THE CLASSROOM

THE TEACHING-LEARNING SITUATION

Modes of teaching and learning in the classroom offered further insights into the image that the instructors hoped the recruit would inculcate. The classroom situation is particularly important to discuss, since it was there that the recruit spent most of his day. The typical classroom situation seemed to be based on the traditional setting in which a teacher talked and students quietly listened at their desks. Even the goals of the classes seemed to parallel those of the traditional style of training—the accumulation of subject matter and the memorization of facts. In addition, the assumption of discipline usually associated with the "old guard" classroom setting was in evidence. Explained one instructor to the class:

> We harass you because we know the requirements you
> need. . . . We are trying to develop objective people who can
> think situations through . . . we have to impose our authority
> on you to get you to know how to respond to situations and
> rationally deal with a situation.

Discipline was not only a necessary force for the cultivation of rationality and objectivity; it also seemed to be a necessary force for motivating the recruit to learn his lessons. "I'm sorry we have to bear down on you, but we have to watch over you like this in order for this training to have an impact on you."

The instructors might not have been too far off the mark when they assumed the recruit needed an external source of authority. Perhaps the recruit accepted his relatively passive role in the classroom because he placed little worth in "book learning."[10] If the recruit par-

---

[10] Joseph Kadish, "Mental Health Training of the Police," *Mental Hygiene*, 50 (April 1966), pp. 205–211.

ticipated in lectures at all, it was usually to ask questions of clarification. When instructors extended their classes into the coffee break time, he became noticeably restless and squirmed noisily in his seat in order to politely indicate that they were going beyond their "allotted" time.

To the recruit it seemed that on-the-job training was more practical than classroom learning: one learns by doing, not by listening. He appeared wary of the scholar who might perform well in the classroom but who would be unable to be depended on in field situations. Lectures that offered practical tools for police work were valued (such as role plays, law, and how to effect a legal arrest), but lectures that seemed unrelated to the necessities of field work were ignored. Indeed, most of the recruits seemed to think that they learned more about police work in one week of field experience than in the previous six weeks of classes, as the following statements indicate.

You find out that what you learn in the academy isn't so; it's a waste of time.

I learned more on the precinct in one week than I did here.

I'm glad I saw how things were really done. If we followed the book, we'd never make any arrests.

To what extent these statements reflected the recruit's true attitudes regarding academy training is debatable. To give an outward sign that the academy did not fit into the needs of the officer in the field seemed acceptable among the recruits; perhaps it was even expected by them. In contrast, when he was alone, a recruit told me, "I know I wouldn't like to go straight on the job without some background." And when I passed out a questionnaire asking the recruits to evaluate their training for field work, 31 of the 52 recruits who filled them out gave positive responses; thus, one should be cautious in forming any generalizations.

If the recruit was biased against classroom training, some of the instructors, though by no means typical, seemed to be also. However, the recruit tended to accept their comments as being more realistic than those of the majority of instructors.

. . . don't worry about that now. Wait till you get out of the academy. In here, we stick by the book.

There are tricks of the trade we can't teach you in the academy, but you'll learn them.

These sparse comments seemed to have such an impact on the recruit that he believed that many of his classes were either irrelevant or misrepresentative, for example, Community Relations classes. It appeared that the recruit perceived the academy program as an initial phase of training that he would have to tolerate for a few months.

If he was expected to sit quietly for six or seven hours a day, the recruit seemed to feel that the instructors should, at least, make their lectures entertaining. The need for a gimmick was recognized by one recruit who said, pointing to an instructor:

Doesn't he look like Jonathan Winters? Look at the way he walks. He's really funny. All he'd have to say was "Hello," "Good-bye" [he accompanied the words with the comedian's mannerisms], and he'd have the whole class listening to what he says. Here he comes; look at the way he walks.

Here, at least, the staff and most of the instructors seemed to agree with the recruit: a gimmick was needed for each class if the recruits were to pay attention to them. There were two general techniques that they used to capture the interest of the recruit. Sexual jokes during the lecture was one technique. Hardly a lecture went by without some off-color joke. A second method used by instructors who accompanied their lectures with slides was to intersperse the slide collection with pictures of nudes. As the nudes flicked across the screen, the recruit's attentiveness, shifting positions, and craning neck contrasted sharply with his earlier sedateness.

In addition to the more general techniques, a few lecturers tried to motivate the class to learn their material in more specific ways. Often it was said that the knowledge in question would protect the recruit from embarrassment, departmental discipline, or lawsuits once he left the academy. For example, in a lecture on arrests, the recruit was admonished with:

Baby, you better learn this, or your ass will be in the sling! . . .

If you don't know the elements of the law, you'll end up looking like a fool or even lose your case.

More notable were the department's formal incentives to encourage the recruit to perform well during academy training. The awards sponsored by police organizations such as the Detectives Association and the Police Brotherhood Association were established specifically to induce "professionalization" among the recruits. An off-duty gun worth $60, required of all departmental members, was presented at graduation to each of the two recruits with the highest overall average in the academy written examinations and to the recruit with the highest firearms average score. The recruit with the second highest firearms average received a $25 savings bond. A $500 scholarship toward tuition for a police science degree was awarded to the recruit selected by the staff for his all-around excellence.

Interestingly, three of the five prizes awarded, in the words of the staff, to "encourage professionalization" were revolvers—especially since the revolver appeared to be an important symbol of the police image for the recruit. During the first day of the session, the recruit was warned, "If you can't shoot a gun, you shouldn't be here." Of all the skills necessary in police work, it was the officer's marksmanship that was periodically evaluated throughout his career. If an officer lost his accuracy, he lost his right to be a policeman. "You must be checked out with firearms once a year, and occasionally we have to drop somebody for this."

Thus it seemed that the intellectual competence image of the policeman was superseded by an action image. While the recruit wore weaponry within two weeks of the session, the training was two-thirds over before he received his wallet-sized card with the Miranda warnings (see p. 102). One instructor remarked, "They give you a gun but not [the Miranda cards]. Well, people like to see a police officer with a gun." Unfortunately, then, the public also identifies the gun with the policeman. In any case, perhaps the department was expressing in another unrecognized way through its training methods the kind of image it really had in mind when it claimed to be developing professional police officers.

ETHIC OF MASCULINITY

As in many predominantly male occupations, there were ribald jokes, profanities, and boasts about sexual encounters throughout the academy session. However, it appeared that these displays of masculinity went beyond mere joking, swearing, and boasting. They seemed to show to the recruit that he was, indeed, among men and thereby testified to his own manhood. The phrase "ethic of masculinity" refers to the apparent need of the recruit to confirm his masculine image to others and to himself by exaggerating the characteristics associated with manhood. These characteristics include physical and sexual prowess, courage, profanity, and aggression toward authority.[11]

The man-of-action image, emanating from the ethic of masculinity, seemed to be an important but implicit component of the professional

---

[11] Jackson Toby, "Violence and the Masculine Ideal: Some Qualitative Data," *Annals*, 364 (March 1966), pp. 19–27.

image. The recruit seemed to perceive the police officer as a man of action with the emphasis both on the *man* of action and the man of *action*. A police officer was physically strong, virile, and courageous. Less inclined to depend on persuasion through discourse, he would rely on physical force. Not afraid of dangerous work, his code of loyalty included putting his life "on the line" in order to help a fellow officer. The recruit who did not manifest the man-of-action image was not as highly esteemed by his fellow classmates, and he certainly was not accessible to the inner circles.

In one case in particular, the recruit class expressed disapproval when it thought some fellow recruits were rejecting the image of the policeman as a man of action. It occurred after an announcement that the class was to participate in a murder investigation. This was the first opportunity the class had had to leave the classroom situation for "real" police work. However, the academy staff needed six men to remain behind to help move some furniture. The reaction of the group as the volunteers left ranks was a friendly but critical hissing as if the six men were not making the proper response as police officers.

Sometimes the image of the officer in action had its humorous spots. One example occurred when an alert recruit became suspicious (over a weekend).

> I was parked in my car when I saw a man slink along the side
> of the drug store and then turn and go around the back. Thinking
> I was on to something, I got out and went around the other side.
> The guy was taking a leak!

The second incident occurred during Field Week. The sergeant asked if anybody had a family call during his tour of duty. About ten hands went up, and a voice spoke softly, "I responded to one call; I ran around the back [of the house] and the dog got me."

In contrast, the police academy image, in which a recruit passively sits at his desk while listening to a lecturer and whose spit-shined leatherwork turns him into a "patent leather soldier," ran against the grain of the recruit. To be a "good" recruit implied a docility and childlike conformity that contradicted the man-of-action image. Consequently, the recruit rejected, through subtle acts of rebellion, the image intentionally or unintentionally defined by the academy. During drill a recruit pushed the man in front of him, who almost collided with the recruit in front of him. One recruit pulled out the back of another recruit's shirt while still another recruit grabbed someone else's memo book and let it drop to the floor. During inspection, ties were pulled off and shirts were pulled out. Instead of running through riot exercises, some recruits danced or walked whenever the instructor's back was turned. Class breaks and lunch hour afforded more time for the men to pull off ties and pull out memo books or blackjacks from otherwise smartly dressed recruits. Once someone placed a blackjack in my empty holster (I was never allowed to carry police weaponry), which I interpreted as a show of disdain for the police academy image.[12] Manliness, then, may also have involved a defiance against leaders and authority; for total conformity meant that one surrendered his freedom to act as an individual.

Physical prowess was esteemed as part of the man-of-action image. On the other hand, mental action seemed not to be defined as action at all, since more prestige was attached to performing well on the pistol range and playing football during coffee breaks than to doing well on written examinations on class lectures. In fact, my willingness and capacity to play football contributed toward my acceptance as a "regular guy." As one recruit remarked to me as we played football during a lunch period, "When you first came, I thought you were a canary-ass brain—you know, those smart guys."

Off-color jokes, profanity, and stories heard or experienced in the military or in police work were typical of many group discussions. The jokes, the use of profanity, and the tales about sexual encounters seemed to confirm the manhood of the recruit. It appeared important for a recruit to confirm his masculinity by contributing some jokes of his own, but lacking these, he should laugh robustly with those recruits who did. In each case, ribald jokes were aggressive toward someone or something, usually an out-group. Many times a police officer was the protagonist, in which case the male made his conquest. Male protagonists who were not policemen turned out to be naive, stupid, or cuckholds.

You ever hear about the guy who always wanted to be a cop?
He could never pass a test, so he bought a uniform and whistle.
He's having fun until a broad asks him for directions, but she asks him to get into the car. He gets in, and she strips—she's got a pair of 44's . . . "Go ahead," she says, "touch 'em." "Uh, there's just one thing lady, I ain't a real cop."

Conversations, such as the following, never failed to draw a group of attentive recruits. "Experienced recruits," those who had served in

---

[12] These behaviors may be aptly applied to Erving Goffman's concept of role distance in *Encounters* (Indianapolis: Bobbs-Merrill, 1961), pp. 84–152.

other police departments, shared some of their encounters with females in the past—all in the line of duty. In this example, several recruits were discussing their experiences patrolling areas of parked lovers.

R_1: He [his partner] was a fucking sadist. He'd wait until they were stripped, and then he'd rush up and pull them out of the car. He was really a sadist.

R_2: We'd wait till dark, and then we would go around hoping to catch some couple.

R_3: I know a guy who used to crawl into the ventilating units of the toilets . . . .

The "raw recruits" offered stories heard from their brothers or friends who were police officers or who were themselves abused with their dates. For instance, one recruit claimed that his brother found a parked couple heavily petting. After he comically illustrated how the couple must have tried to cover themselves, he said his brother began questioning them and then chatting with them. After a while, the boy fell asleep, so his brother and the half-naked girl went to the patrol car where he remained with her for most of the night. The listening recruits dreamily sighed to each other as they possibly envisioned themselves in similar circumstances. At the very least, they expressed the enviable position in which this recruit's brother had found himself.

The acting out of the ethic of masculinity may indicate why police officers tend to react personally to an affront on police authority. It would seem that an officer would be less likely to react to disrespect personally if he feels secure with himself. Concomitantly, it would be those officers least secure in their masculine image who are prone to react violently to perceived threats to their masculinity. Thus, while William Westley suggests that violence by police officers emerges when they perceive threats to their authority, he does not appear to go far enough.[13] What people may be doing when they challenge an officer's authority is to challenge his masculinity which he, in part, identifies with authority and respect.

Dirty workers probably place as much esteem on their occupations

[13] William A. Westley, "Violence and the Police," *American Journal of Sociology*, 49 (August 1953), pp. 34–41. See also, Arthur E. Hippler, "The Game of Black and White at Hunters Point," *Trans-Action*, 7 (April 1970), pp. 56-63.

as do other members of the community. Although some dirty workers see their work as a calling, I suspect that most know that they are doing dirty work. Some may try to romanticize their work, but underneath their bravado may be resentment about their work and an envy of "clean" workers. Certainly this was true among the police recruits. Consequently, the dirty worker, in his low self-esteem, may embrace the ethic of masculinity, but not necessarily because he is insecure about his manhood. Rather he embraces it because, if he is nothing else, he is at least a man. Many men can rationalize away their limitations, their subservience, and their lack of prestige, but few can calmly ignore threats or ridicules about their masculinity.

In the case of the recruit, the public may have defined his total identity as "cop," as dirty worker. But the recruit seemed to be saying through his ethic of masculinity that while he was indeed a "cop," it was only a subidentity. First and foremost, he was a man. The recruit and dirty worker exaggeration of masculine characteristics may merely be an affirmation that although they do someone else's dirty work, they are still men.

RECRUIT REACTION

The way in which the staff and lecturers seemed to define professionalism, how they expressed the concept to the recruit, and the kind of image the recruit might have expected the department to formally and informally reward once he was in the field have been outlined. Nevertheless, I have been able to offer relatively little data on the recruit's perspectives toward professionalism outside of his notion of the man of action. This sparse information is probably the result of two factors. First, the lecture on professionalism partly quoted earlier in the chapter seemed to articulate what the recruit was thinking himself. Second, the matter appeared to him to be out of his hands: the potential for police officers to be professional was there, the difference rested with the community. As one recruit said angrily, "How can you be professional when you stop someone and he spits in your face?"

With all the instruction on professionalism, what was really meant by the staff remained vague in the mind of the recruit. To him, professionalism seemed to be something that was described in the cogent speech on professionalism; it implied dedication to one's duty, a conservative and respectful appearance, integrity, courtesy, and self-control. Still, there was no clear presentation of just what a professional was. For example, notice the lack of continuity in one statement.

> We're professional, and we can't do our work in a slip-shod
> fashion. We have to follow the [Rules and Procedures]. I don't
> care what it is, use common sense and good judgment, and
> nobody will burn your ass.

At first professionalism meant performing one's work neatly by follow-ing established rules and procedures. This was followed immediately by confidence in common sense as the policeman's most precious tool—but only because the recruit would be able to protect himself from departmental or other external criticisms!

There were a few times, however, when the recruit offered hints at what the term "professionalism" meant to him. Early in the session, I overheard the following stories.

> One cop walked into a bank being robbed. He was in plain
> clothes, so he acted like a scared chicken . . . he backed away,
> cowering and yelling, "Don't shoot, don't shoot!" One of the two
> robbers came over and said, "Cool it, take it easy; you won't get
> hurt." When the robber lifted his arm to hit him, the cop had a gun
> pointed right between his eyes.

> There was one cop in a gun battle. He fired twice, immediately
> reloaded, then shot four more times. The guy came out saying,
> "You're out of bullets," and the cop drilled him.

The remark made by one recruit who heard these stories was "They're more professional than we are." Then he added gravely, "You really have to be sharp to get the drop on them." It appeared that to be a professional, an officer had to have the capacity to out-think, outwit, or outmaneuver his opponent.[14]

One of the recruits from Megopolis Police Department offered another perspective on professionalism. A fellow recruit asked him if he thought the police in Rurban County were more professional than those in the city. He replied that he thought there was a better attitude among the men in Rurban County, but that the difference may simply have been because the city force was too large for the individual to count. Then he said, "I don't know; I'll have to find out when I'm brought up on something and see how I'm backed up."

---

[14] Walter B. Miller, "Lower Class Culture as a Generating Milieu of Gang Delinquency," *Journal of Social Issues*, 14 (1958), pp. 5–19, discusses the focal concern of "smart-ness" in this sense of conning, outwitting, and duping.

For him, professionalism meant support from his superiors in the event that departmental or public charges were placed against him. In his hierarchy of professional values, in-group solidarity seemed to come first.

The image that the recruit desired for himself and for law enforcement seemed to be personified by a visiting lecturer, a member of the Jordanian State Police. The recruit appeared to be very much impressed by the power, prestige, and the assumed competence of the typical Jordanian police officer. His salary was twice that of a school teacher's. He had the power to arrest on mere suspicion, and he could obtain permission to search private property by a phone call to the district attorney. If the officer were knowledgeable in law, he was permitted to prosecute his own case.

Apparently just as impressive to the recruit was the high clearance rate and very low crime rate. The reasons given by the lecturer for this success were strict laws and complete cooperation from the people. In the words of the Jordanian:

There is complete cooperation between police officer and people.
If there is a crime and no police officer is around, people will tell
all. We solve 95% of cases. We have no robbery and murder.
We have low rate of crime because of strict laws, severe
sentences, and no mercy. There is no parole system. Hanging
is the death sentence . . . Narcotics is ten to fifteen years.
["Beautiful!" cried a recruit.]

Following the class, some recruits compared the American legal system with Jordan's.

R₁: How do you like that in Jordan and with the police state—
throw the guy in on suspicion.

R₂: That'll never work in America.

R₃: (regretfully) No, no, it'll never work.

When I asked the latter recruit if he would prefer a police state in America, he answered: "No, not that, but cooperation from the people would be good; imagine, they solve 95 percent of their crime and they don't have much of that!" Living in a society that seemed permissive toward criminals and suspicious toward police officers, the recruits must have thought that the Jordanian police image was ideal.

Thus the general reaction of the recruit class to the whole question of professionalism appeared to be, "Yes, we are professional, but the public doesn't treat us as such," or "if we are not now professional, we could be if the public would get involved in law enforcement and the courts would support our judgment as experts," or "if the public wants professionals, they'll have to pay more." Therefore, it was useless to debate the issue of police professionalism, since the problem appeared to be basically beyond their control. If there was anything to be done, it was to educate the public that they ought to treat the police as professionals.

LAW AND THE PROFESSIONAL IMAGE

If it is assumed that a person's self-image is closely linked to the organizational structure in which he operates from day to day, then the professional image that seems an integral part of academy training has behavioral and attitudinal outcomes. Since the patrolman is associated with law enforcement, it is necessary to explore the consequences that a recruit's training may have on his conception of the law; this subject is the focus of the remainder of the chapter. The last two major out-groups—lawyers and judges—will be considered in this connection.

LAW AS MORALITY

The law seemed to represent two perspectives to the recruit: guidelines that the officer can use to protect himself from charges of malfeasance or incompetence (as discussed in the previous chapter); and principles of morality. Law, as a set of moral principles that members of a community are obligated to obey, is best discussed in connection with the recruit's image of himself as a morally superior professional. The recruit seemed to think that, since the law was morality per se, it was only just that a violator of the law should be punished according to the seriousness of the offense. Those who guarded, respected, or enforced the law were moral persons. Those who broke or disrespected the law, or who allowed offenders to break the law without the proper degree of punishment, ranged from the less moral to the absolutely immoral. Based on the lessons that he learned in the academy, the recruit appeared to define himself as a moral caretaker of society. Lawyers and judges were often defined as immoral because they made and supported the ground rules of law enforcement that seemed more protective of the rights of the offender than the right of the victim to have the offender properly punished.

It appeared that the basis for this perceived distinction between the recruit and the legal profession in the hierarchy of morality was based on qualitative differences in the law. There are two types of law: substantive law and procedural law. Substantive law defines what behavior may be handled by the legal system. Procedural law is composed of rules that govern how a person who breaks substantive law should be processed through the legal system by police officers and officers of the court.

For the most part, it was the substantive law which the recruit seemed to identify with the morality of the community, as an end in itself. Procedural law was perceived more as a set of prescriptions that interfered with the attainment of justice, that is, the proper punishment of a violation of law. Those who would place procedural law before the primacy of substantive law were seen as immoral, since this reasoning could result in a violator's being only minimally punished if punished at all. Since judges and lawyers operate under the primacy of procedural law (in accordance with the American value of presuming innocence until guilt has been proven), the recruit seemed to perceive them as subverters of law, order, and justice. Nevertheless, judges and lawyers had the last word in the matter, since they controlled the framework of legal activity and established the rules that had to be followed. As a result, the recruit found himself competing with other members of the legal system over the legitimate definition of justice. This did not mean that the recruit (or the patrolman) did not believe in due process of law, for he did. He objected, however, to the "obvious" manipulation of due process for the purpose of restraining the enforcement of substantive law which often allowed an offender to escape punishment.

The recruit's perspectives to both procedural law and substantive law were not without ambivalence. In the previous chapter it was pointed out that the recruit and probably the patrolman would tend to overlook procedural law if they felt threatened. Substantive law was not so simply defined as rules of morality either. At least two recruits thought that the laws prohibiting the use of marijuana should be relaxed, and several others questioned the legality of laws against abortion. Finally, what the recruit and his instructors did not seem to recognize was that police lobbies often opposed attempts at legal reform whether it was substantive or procedural.[15]

[15] Ed Cray, "Criminal Interrogations and Confessions: The Ethical Imperative," *Wisconsin Law Review* (1968), pp. 173–183.

To sum up, the recruit seemed to believe that his interpretation of justice, that is, punishment which fits the crime, was one that was more just and humane than a lawyer's or judge's. What could be more just than having a person's violator pay for his misconduct? Several times a recruit complained to me privately or to an instructor during class that the oath he took on entering the academy was "useless," not because he lacked the willingness or capacity to abide by it, but because legal barriers made it inapplicable. According to this view, the problem of law enforcement did not lie so much within the police profession, as it did with lawyers and judges. Indeed, the recruit seemed to believe that lawyers unscrupulously distorted the law while judges encouraged them to do so by providing them the means via their rulings.

PROSTITUTES OF THE LAW

THE LAWYER. The lawyer seemed to be defined as someone who would deliberately circumvent the law to save a client from a conviction. The client's guilt or innocence would be of no consequence as long as the lawyer received his fee. As Skolnick observed in his study, judges sometimes postponed a case with the implicit understanding that the request was made because of the client's inability to pay at that time.[16]

The lawyer's claim that he was merely conforming to procedural law was belied by some of his tactics in and out of court. For instance, police officers seemed to believe that legislators sometimes constructed the law in ways that would be helpful to their own ends instead of to the community's. As one instructor put it, "The legislators ... are lawyers, and they are writing the law knowing that they may have to defend a client in court."

Although such a charge is an exaggeration, the behavior of lawyers once in court seemed to offer substantial evidence to the recruit that lawyers subordinated the needs of the community to their own. For example, the recruit seemed to believe that harmony between the police and the community often was disrupted by a lawyer.

We had one time when things were bad in a community, so we

[16] Jerome H. Skolnick, *Justice Without Trial*, p. 189.

brought in all the drunks or people with bottles in their hands. All the people were happy; the problems were decreased significantly. The community was satisfied, and we stuck out our chests. What happened? Some smart lawyer was crying "unconstitutional," and now everything is as bad as it was.

The lawyer could not claim he was really interested in observing the law by placing procedural law or the "spirit of the law" as primary among the legal values. It seemed that he was concerned about neither procedure nor spirit. Certainly the recruit appeared to think that the lawyer in the following anecdote was not trying to enforce the "spirit of the law" for the good of the client or for the community.

"Person" does not just mean the body, but it can mean an individual, a public or private corporation, and now, an unincorporated association. It seems some bright lawyer got a client off by saying that an unincorporated association did not apply to the law as it stood on the books.

In reference to procedural law, it was interesting to notice that according to an assistant district attorney, the complaints of lawyers regarding the rights of their clients had changed as the laws had changed. Instructors claimed that charges of police brutality were declining rapidly because of the new procedural laws. Defense attorneys no longer search for police abuse of their clients; some do not even question whether or not the prescribed warnings were given to the suspect. The first question the attorney seems to ask his client is if he *understood* the warnings. An instructor claimed that the county lost a one-half million dollar arson case because "now the act is they're stupid."

The sudden change of the defense attorney's charges from police brutality to nonadvisement of legal rights tended to cast doubt on the previous claims of police brutality. Undoubtedly, instances of police brutality occurred, but it might have been that the rates of brutality were inflated by false but strategic charges by lawyers and clients.[17] Judges, including those on the United States Supreme Court, were criticized by instructors and recruits for making rulings that allowed and supported further circumvention of substantive law.

[17] P. Chevigny, *Police Power* (New York: Pantheon, 1969); and Ed Cray, *The Big Blue Line* (New York: Coward-McCann, 1967) for opposing views.

JUDGES AND COURTS OF LAW. If the recruit's feeling of moral superiority relative to judges did not stem directly from his conception of the law as a moral order (which dichotomized people into the moral and the immoral), his fellow recruits and instructors provided him with other convincing arguments for questioning the common sense of judges.

We have what we call the Supreme Court of [District Court].
(Laughter) Now we call them the Supreme Court because they
have twelve individual judges, each with his own opinion.
(Laughter) The U.S. Supreme Court is no different, except they
have more room.

The instructors further attacked the probity of the members of the United States Supreme Court by questioning their qualifications compared to RCPD candidate requirements.

How do you become a Supreme Court Justice today? Well, you
go to law school, practice law for three years, and then you go
into public office. Then you get appointed Supreme Court
Justice—never having rubbed shoulders with a rookie, the D.A.'s,
the judges at District Court (although *that* may be okay)—our
own Earl Warren.

Since the standards of selection to the United States Supreme Court were presented as being very lax, it came as no surprise when the recruit learned that county, district, state, and national courts deviated from their intended "moral purposes." "Did you ever see that lady blindfolded, holding the scales in District Court? If she ever saw what went on in District Court, she'd throw away the scales."

If the recruit still doubted the moral standing of judges, there was the coup de grâce. An instructor informed the recruit class that a couple of years ago the State Supreme Court initiated an investigation of the county's district courts because "it was believed that the District Court was not policing itself." A judge from Megopolis City was consequently appointed to supervise the courts. Thus the recruit seemed to realize that judges, the same ones who were responsible for castigating police officers in court, were so corrupt that their own colleagues from other districts had to supervise them. This knowledge permitted the recruit to place much of the blame for ineffective law enforcement on the courts.

One instructor suggested that the problem of law enforcement could be remedied once the policeman educated the judges. In the case of radar traps, for instance, he claimed that the county was winning 70 percent of its cases because it taught judges how radar worked and that, even without radar, police officers were able to make reasonable estimates of speeds.

Indeed, there were times when it seemed that the recruit thought that the intelligence of the judge was insufficient to enable him to absorb fully the testimony that he heard. When discussing a car stealing ring that specialized in Cadillacs, an instructor mentioned the problem of obtaining court support of police efforts. The county had charged a lawyer with the receiving of stolen goods because he had gone to a bar in a slum area and had bought a Cadillac at half its market value. The presiding judge, the recruit was told, acquitted the lawyer, for "how would he know the car was stolen?"

An experience of a recruit from Megopolis Department further illustrated the recruit's sense of frustration in the light of such apparent judicial astigmatism.

> I brought a guy in for cock-sucking, and the judge dismissed it
> because he couldn't believe two men would do that. The judge
> asked me how long I observed them doing that. Well, it takes
> only two seconds to see what's going on, but I said ten seconds
> because he wouldn't have believed me for only two seconds. He
> dismissed the case because he wouldn't believe they did it at all!

The recruit may have explained away court actions as a consequence of unqualified, naive, and probably some very stupid judges. What he did not seem sensitive to were the different experiences of the police officer and the judge that accounted for their conflicting perspectives.[18] The officer assumes that a man whom he arrests is guilty or he would not have arrested him in the first place; therefore, it is irrational to assume his innocence or to release him. While the judge may see a new face standing in front of him, the officer may have been lenient with the offender in the past. Defining his job as enforcing the law, the officer perceives procedural law as counterproductive. In contrast, the judge defines due process of law as essential to the American legal system: what is a technicality for the policeman is a fundamental principle for the judge. Because of heavy calendars and poor administration, judges are forced to make quick decisions; they rely on dismissals to reduce the chances of injustice to the defendant. None of these issues were presented to the recruit

---

[18] Jerome H. Skolnick, *Justice Without Trial*, pp. 182–203; James Q. Wilson, *Varieties of Police Behavior* (Cambridge: Harvard University, 1968), pp. 50–52.

in an enlightened manner. On the other hand, neither the public nor the courts seem to recognize that it is the police officer who must bear the psychological burden for the court's problems.

Much of the apparent animosity of the recruit toward judges seemed to revolve around court decisions that "allowed" violators of the law to escape punishment, set up rigid guidelines for police activity, and freed known criminals on mere technicalities. Perhaps no other Supreme Court decision was more vilified by the recruit and his instructors than the Miranda decision.

NEUTRALIZATION OF LAW ENFORCEMENT

BENT JUSTICE. The Miranda decision stated that persons in the custody of the police should be informed by a police officer of their right to remain silent and their right to legal counsel even if they could not afford one. The Miranda decision, which applied to the questioning period of police investigations, extended the Escobedo decision of 1964, which held that a defendant in a felony case had the right to counsel once he appeared in court even if he could not afford a lawyer. The instructors seemed to dispel any doubts in the mind of the recruit as to whether the Miranda decision was in the best interests of law, order, or justice.

> Not even the Supreme Court knew what it was doing [in the Escobedo decision]. They said there is a period between investigation and suspicion during which he is entitled to a lawyer. We asked them what they meant, where do you draw the line? Silence. Well, we thought the situation would be okay in a couple of years. They fixed it okay. (Laughter) The Miranda decision, and they shocked the country again. We warn them of their rights. Now we tell them we'll give you a lawyer if you can't afford it. . . . We get them back. But what bothers me is the overall effect on law enforcement.

Apparently, the feeling was that once a client obtained a lawyer whose only concern was to free him, there would be little chance of eliciting any information, much less a confession. The first thing the lawyer would do would be to instruct his client not to say a word and to inform the investigating officers that they were not to question his client. Since, the instructors claim, the only way to solve a crime is to question the suspect, if he either wants a lawyer or he does not understand his rights "you've lost him." The substantial number of cases cleared by confessions could then be expected to decline (in spite of evidence to the contrary).[19] The decline might encourage others to try to break the law.

Even if the Miranda warnings are given to a suspect who agrees to relinquish his rights, the police officer must attend a Huntley hearing. It is a formal judicial hearing that determines whether the suspect waived his rights voluntarily or whether he was apprised of them at all. "Yes, I give up my Constitutional rights; yes, I believe in God; yes, I want to talk; yes, I want to be serached. Then you get a Huntley investigation to see if the waiver is legal."

It appeared to the recruit that lawyers and judges did not want substantive law effectively enforced, since they continued to curtail police discretion. For instance, police officers seemed to believe that wiretapping, judiciously supervised, could be an effective tool of law enforcement. Although they admitted wiretapping infringed on individual rights, they felt that the rights of the community should take precedence in the wake of the apparent power of organized crime. The ruling of the Supreme Court on wiretapping seemed not only unrealistic, but inane: the police must warn those who are supposed to be secretly investigated. "You can tap his phone, but you tell him."

Because of procedural law, many known criminals, including murderers, could not be brought to trial or convicted. The Miranda decision seemed to benefit only the guilty.

> As far as I am concerned, the Miranda decision does not help the
> innocent person. It helps the guilty person. No sane person
> without torture is going to confess to a crime he did not commit.
> And evidence through torture was never admissible long before
> the Miranda decision.

Thus, the Supreme Court rulings not only seemed to reduce the effectiveness of law enforcement, they seemed unnecessary to the interests of justice. The belief of both recruit and instructor appeared to be that police agents were disproportionately rebuked and controlled compared to other segments of the legal system. A recruit's complaint that police mistakes wind up in a Supreme Court ruling while nothing happens to incompetent judges or lawyers who "twist the facts" raises an interesting point. Kai Erikson observes that the

---

[19] Arthur Niederhoffer, *Behind the Shield*, pp. 161–164, cites several findings that the Miranda decision has affected the rates of clearance only minutely, and that confessions clear only 10 percent of the cases anyway.

normative boundaries of a society or group (the values that differentiate one group from another) are forever being tested to determine
what degree of variation from the norms will be tolerated by the
group members.[20] Although the result is often a "rubber band" effect
in which the boundaries "bounce back" to the status quo, such is not
the case with the police. The police test the limits of their legal boundaries but, since these boundaries do not bounce back to their original
state, they find that court actions increasingly *lessen* their areas of
activity.

Not only was police discretion seriously hampered, the courts
seemed intent on protecting the criminal—even to the extent of grant-
ing him immunity from informers and undercover surveillance. The
recruit was told about a detective who received a phone call giving the
location of the sales of illegal drugs. The next night the detective went
to the location and arrested a drug peddler who was selling drugs
"right out in the open." The peddler was acquitted, not because the
information was false, but because the Supreme Court ruled that a
police informer must be one whose reliability has already been tested.
The phone caller did not qualify as a police informer.

> They wanted our undercover agents to give the Miranda
> warnings. (Laughter) No kidding. I asked the judge, "Why?
> The Miranda decision was for custodial interrogation." The judge
> said, "Well, I don't read it that way." "What case did you get it
> from?" "Well, I never read the whole thing." (Laughter) That's
> what we're up against.

The recruit seemed unable to understand why the criminal merited
such protection. It seemed as if one's personal rights included the
right to commit a crime without suffering the full consequences.

As if the Supreme Court decisions were not bad enough, local
judges seemed to free violators of the law on relatively minor technicalities. It seemed a clear case of finding small technical points in the
law to guarantee that the police officer would not win a conviction.

> The one thing I like is for a rookie to write out a lot of summonses
> because he'll have to go to court, and he'll learn. One fellow lost
> a case because he didn't know the dimensions of a speed sign.
> He knew what it said, but it was thrown out of court. Don't ask
> me why.

[20] Kai Erikson, *Wayward Puritans* (New York: John Wiley, 1966).

The recruit seemed to believe that the courts were diametrically opposed to the principles of law, order, and justice. His belief appeared to be reinforced when he learned that judges seemed hesitant to convict a person even when the suspect was clearly guilty.

This is what will bust your balls—the courts. Our Narcotics Squad is doing very well, making good arrests, good evidence, and then they let him plead fourth degree misdemeanor. For what?

Because he's a student!

A recruit from Megopolis Department confirmed the apparent court injustice. He had arrested two youths for smoking marijuana. The judge dismissed both defendants, one because he was going to college and the other because he was going into the army. Such permissiveness by the courts toward the criminal, assumed the recruit, could only bring disrespect for the ideals of law and justice. While in the opinion of the recruit and his instructor the courts confused mercy and justice by acquitting defendants, it also appeared that the recruit confused punishment with justice.

Although they were "professionals" responsible for enforcing the moral code of the community, in practice lawyers and judges seemed to leave very little doubt in the mind of the recruit that they were not dedicated to moral values. Hence, they were immoral men. Indeed, what could be more immoral than to leave a victim helpless to have his violator brought to justice?

The ———— Commission has a very starry-eyed view. "A vehicle can be replaced, a life cannot." And they extended it into the home: the home owner cannot even use deadly physical force! So what happens? A thief robs a house. The owner wakes up and says, "You're under arrest," and he says, "Fuck you," and he's gone. When will it all stop?

Considering himself a professional who was expert in law enforcement, the recruit seemed to think that he should be able to use his own judgment as to what would be the right or wrong procedures. According to the law, an officer may search a person only on the grounds of "probable cause" or if he is in personal danger himself. If an officer searches on suspicion only, his case could be "dismissed" even if the searched person was carrying stolen goods.

As one knowledgeable about the behavior of criminals, the recruit generally felt his judgment should not be subjected to examination by the court. State law insists that a conviction must be founded on the principle of "beyond a reasonable doubt." However, if a jury bases its decision on this principle, it implies that the expertise of the officer is questionable. Indeed, the high standards of "beyond a reasonable doubt" could contribute to a defendant's "beating the rap." If respect for the moral code were to be maintained and if police decisions were not to be questioned, the recruits felt that a more "realistic" principle was needed. What seemed to be the solution was stated by a representative of the state liquor authority who announced to them that many of its convictions were upheld because they were based on a principle that enhanced police competence: "A reasonable man would determine from the facts as a trained observer. . . ."

JUSTICE BENT BACK. The image of a professional as competent in his field was probably warped when the recruit became aware that court cases were not won necessarily on their merits. His instructors informed him that lawyers "couldn't get through a case if they stuck to the facts." To win a case, lawyers had to advise their clients never to talk with police officers, and once in court, they tried to discredit the officer in the eyes of the jury. The ways in which the lawyer would try to accomplish the latter, the recruit was warned, were to ignore the facts of the case and to attack the officer's demeanor or educational qualifications. The truth did not win cases. One tactic that the lawyer was said to use in order to discredit the officer was to search for misspelled words or errors in the officer's memo book. That was one reason why the recruit was instructed never to overlap notes of two days on one page and to bring only the relevant pages of the memo book to court.

> It can be embarrassing if you are not sure of your facts. The
> defense attorney may have a piss-poor case, but he makes you
> look ridiculous to the jury. . . . The moment [the memo book] is
> introduced into court, you are vulnerable to any mistakes in it.

In addition, the recruit had to use correct grammar and remain courteous if he were ever placed on the witness stand. "Don't murder the English language. You may have a good case, but it doesn't look good when you testify."

One of the new programs of academy training, beginning with our recruit class, was a field trip to county court. The events included a mock Huntley hearing with the staff of the district attorney's office in which some recruits played the parts of witnesses and the suspect. Thirty minutes into the "hearing," the class became bored and impatient with the constant repetition of questions that appeared to be irrelevant. The next day an instructor pointed out the significance of the long mock hearing.

> I just wanted to talk a little about yesterday in court. I know it
> was tiring, but by God, that's just the way they operate—you

feel when are they going to stop those stupid questions. But "sir"
them to death.

If judges and juries seemed to rely more on appearances than on
the merits of the case, the recruit tended to feel justified to "bend the
law" a little to enforce substantive law and justice. The instructor who
said, "The judge hates you, the DA hates you, the lawyers hate you—
everybody hates you except the defendant," was implying that while
the legal staff was concerned about matters other than justice, the
defendant knew he was where he belonged. When the legal process
seemed to be regulated by immoral persons, it seemed to become the
officer's responsibility to compensate for it. As one recruit mentioned
to me, "When justice bends you one way, we bend it another."

For example, one way in which the Miranda decision could be
countered was to mumble the warnings. If the suspect could not understand the words, that was his misfortune. The important thing was for
the officer to be able to swear truthfully in court that he had given the
warnings. "You don't need to lie—exaggerate." Notice how one
instructor worked in the warning that the suspect is entitled to a
lawyer. He had begun by reading all the warnings to the class.

> Basically that's what you're supposed to say. But when you're
> in the field, try to bullshit them. "Come on, get it off your chest.
> We'll get an attorney for you. Anybody could have done that—
> so you made a mistake."

Thus, substantive law and justice seemed to become identified with
the morality of the community. Procedural law and justice became
rules that hampered law enforcement to the extent that known criminals were allowed to escape the consequences of their actions. As a
professional who was competent in his field, as a moral person who
was concerned about the rectitude of the community, and as one who
had sworn an oath to enforce the law justly, the officer seemed to feel
that he had to maintain some respect for the law in some way. Consequently, countertechniques that had the semblance of conforming to
procedural law in order to assure enforcement of substantive law
seemed to be taught, used, and permitted by members of the police
in-group.

PROFESSIONALISM AS DEFENSIVE

The purpose of this chapter has been to describe and analyze how a
police department defined and took steps to achieve a change in the

image of police work and the self-image of its members. This was carried out by concentrating on one step of the policeman's career—the time he spends at the police academy—and the consequences of that training. Perhaps the role of professionalism in RCPD (and in other police departments) may be brought into better focus if the simple question is asked: Why does the police academy exist at all?

The answer, aside from the obvious need for training, appears to lie in the department's attempt to convince the public (and itself) that police officers are, indeed, professionals. A police officer today is like the teacher of yesterday. He is called on to engage in a variety of services that touch on intimate facets of people's lives. He must make judgments ranging from administration to public relations, from robbery to first aid, and from law to family disputes. The police officer believes that he is an expert in all these services, but he realizes that his competence as a skilled worker is not recognized by the public. He views himself and his department as being constantly challenged to prove their integrity both in and out of court.

Professionalism seems to connote internal competence and freedom from external regulation. The policeman, considering himself an expert in a wide range of services, seems to believe that nobody but another policeman is able to judge accurately his competence or the quality of his service. As Hughes correctly notes, it is the right to make judgments that is most jealously guarded by professional groups.[21] Consequently, it is assumed "all licensed professionals are competent and ethical until found otherwise by their peers." To be able to be judged by one's peers assures the defendant that "occupational experiences" will be taken into account, and for the profession itself means that its members can discuss any mistakes in secret. The threat of an institutional arbiter such as a civilian review board is seen as antiprofessional and as a demand to discuss police secrets openly. Neither aspect is tolerable since, as the eminent sociologist Georg Simmel points out, secrecy fosters group autonomy.[22]

A publicly recognized professional status seems to be perceived as a panacea for most of the ailments plaguing police work. Courts

---

[21] Everett C. Hughes, *Men and Their Work,* pp. 94–95 and 140–142.
[22] Georg Simmel, *The Sociology of Georg Simmel,* edited and translated by Kurt H. Wolff (New York: The Free Press, 1950), pp. 361, 345, 376.

would question police procedures less frequently, and defense attorneys would be less able to resort to trickery or to disparaging the police officer on the witness stand to win their cases. The press would be less inclined to distort news items against the police, and the status of the law enforcement profession would encourage its selection by high calibre men as a career. The public would be supportive of police actions, and its cooperation would decrease the crime rate as well as make budgetary requests, including salary increases, less problematic.

Since professionalism seemed to be the answer to the problems of police work, the first step was to find out what were the characteristics of a profession so that they could strive to meet these criteria. Characteristics were collected from students of professions. Through the years, progressive departments have tried to conform to these criteria. In RCPD, the establishment of a police academy and a police science degree on the college level were supposed to provide evidence to the public that police work involved specialized knowledge and training: not just anybody could be a patrolman. Those who were admitted to the police academy had to pass physical and psychological tests, submit to background investigations, swear an oath to a code of ethics, and successfully meet the requirements of the lengthiest police training in the state. On graduating from the academy, the recruit was licensed by the state to engage in specialized activities. Since experience was necessary to acquire competence and knowledge, there was an informal rule that the first five years of field work were still part of the training.

Law enforcement, it was thought, certainly qualified as a profession, since it was an idealistic and service occupation composed of dedicated men. The characteristics that RCPD lacked were (1) complete group autonomy, and (2) publicly recognized status and prestige. Not only were these conditions extraneous to the quality of the department itself, they also happened to be the very problems that caused the effort toward police professionalization in the first place. Thus, according to the police officer, he qualified as a professional. He had only to convince the public of this.

However, there were problems of definition regarding the professional police officer. It was generally agreed that he was one who was competent in his job and deserved the respect of the public, but beyond that, there was less consensus. Professionalism implied abiding by a code of ethics, performing tactfully and efficiently, looking tidy, earning large salaries, and gaining public cooperation. In prac-

tice, these characteristics became means as well as ends in themselves. The police officer should enforce the law equally and justly;
should perform his job tactfully and efficiently; and should be educated, courteous, and trim *to obtain* complete public cooperation,
higher social status, and salaries comparable to doctors and lawyers.

Because of the nebulous image, the instructors were not sure how
to train in-coming members to become professional. The haziness of
the image was increased by their apparent ambivalence about the
worth of a professional police officer even if one could be trained.
Notwithstanding their desire to train professionals, the instructors
seemed skeptical of the person who did well in the classroom, since
he could be ineffective in field situations. Nevertheless, the need to
acquire the status of a profession was recognized, and the department
simulated the elite professions. Professionals learned in a classroom
setting, so a police academy with its certificate of competence replaced
the apprenticeship training. Professionals had college degrees, so
recruits and patrolmen were encouraged to acquire police science
degrees. In spite of these surface attempts, the orientations of the
academy and the police science curriculum remained essentially
vocational.

The recruit, too, had a funny conception of the professional image.
The only anchorage he could fall back on was not what the instructors
said, but what they did. The instructors' ambivalence about professionalism was carried over to the recruit. On the one hand, they
seemed to want patrolmen who were flexible and independent think-
ers, who were tolerant of other people's attitudes and behavior, who
relied on dialogue and reason rather than on force to achieve order,
and who stressed deliberation. What they taught or reinforced, however, was compliance to authority (which was buttresed by the
organizational structure of the department), and intolerance of other
people's ways of thinking or acting. The value and theory of due
process of law were presented unfavorably or inadequately. Lectures
on marijuana were propagandistic and medically questionable: the
recruit would not be able to talk intelligently on the subject even if
he had wanted to. Role playing was geared to technical proficiency,
not to developing interpersonal skills. Consequently, the recruit was
very receptive towards instructors who claimed that the real training
would occur in the field.

All in all, the image of the patrolman as action-oriented was projected to a significant degree more than the contemplative image.
Professionalism was not identified with intellectual or academic training: it consisted of concrete work situations. The neglect of ideological

changes may help explain why RCPD and other police departments are having such a difficult time in their "convincing process."

The question of how the recruit, the patrolman, and the department adjust to the pressures placed on them by the community and the disparity between what they want and how they are treated will be explored in the following chapter.

..., yet it may be maintained that everyone who
has worn a uniform for many years finds in it a better
organization of life than the man who merely exchanges
one civilian suit in the evening for another civilian
suit during the day ..., for a generic uniform provides
its wearer with a definitive line of demarcation
between his person and the world; it is like a hard
casing against which one's personality and the world
beat sharply and distinctly and are differentiated from
each other; for it is the uniform's true function to ...
conceal whatever in the human body is soft and flowing,
covering up the soldier's underclothes and skin. ...
Hermann Broch, The Sleepwalkers

Depersonalization.

CHAPTER FIVE

DEPERSONALIZATION AND DEFENSIVE BUREAUCRACY

Unlike the themes of defensiveness and professionalization, the theme of depersonalization connotes a pattern of thinking and acting that was neither explicitly stated nor recognized by the recruit or his instructors. Nevertheless, I believe this third and last theme captures an important motif of police thinking and behavior. Although the use of the term "depersonalization" may be questioned, I shall try to justify my choice in the next several pages. In the course of the chapter, it will become clear that other concepts such as stereotypy and impersonalization are components of depersonalization. Perhaps some people would prefer the word "dehumanization" instead of depersonalization, but by using the latter term, I hope to avoid the philosophical and moral implications usually associated with the former one. Rather than defining depersonalization in any definitive way, my purpose is to convey a subjective sense of what the term may mean to the recruit and how it seemed to be manifested in academy training.

Since "depersonalization" is not a common term in sociological literature, a brief explanation of its use here is called for. The concept of depersonalization has been employed predominantly by psychiatrists and existential therapists to convey a sense of self-estrangement, of a person who experiences a part of the self as something alien to

113

him.[1] With the notable exception of Helen Merrell Lynd, this connotation is limited because it tends to neglect the interaction between the person and the social environment that may contribute to or impede depersonalization.[2] This does not mean that psychiatry totally excludes the social environment from its analysis, but it does seem to subordinate its impact to intraindividual processes. That is, psychiatry, like psychology, places its emphasis on what subjectively impinges on ego. I wish to extend depersonalization to include the two-way action between ego and alter, or the social structure. Ego not only responds to alter, but alter responds to ego's response which, in turn, affects ego's subsequent response, and so forth. In this framework, depersonalism becomes a psychostructural variable instead of carrying only the essentially psychological connotation it has held in the past. It focuses on the interaction between the person, the cultural norms available to him, and the social structure, including his occupational organization.

For the purpose of this discussion, depersonalization represents both a state of mind and the basis for defining the quality of interaction between individuals. It is characterized by categorizing persons and interacting with them on the basis of these categories rather than on each actor's individual merits. By categorization is meant the tendency of the person to oversimplify by dichotomizing issues into black-and-white terms and by stereotyping. He also defines himself as part of a category devoid of any individuality and thereby comes to perceive himself as an object that is more acted upon than acting. Consequently, he becomes impersonal and uninvolved—an automaton whose personal feelings must be suppressed and whose actions are calculated. Not only does he perceive himself as an object rather than a person, he thinks others perceive him similarly and that they treat him in line with that perception. Incapable of empathizing with people of different molds than himself, he perceives others as objects to be manipulated. On the other hand, not to be depersonal means to be one's self in all its multifaceted splendor and mediocrity, to perceive others as multifaceted, and to refrain from treating others in stereotypical or dichotomous terms. Concomitantly, it includes the belief that others perceive one as an individual and treat one as such.

[1] Frederick A. Weiss, "Self-Alienation: Dynamics and Therapy," *American Journal of Psychoanalysis*, 21 (1961), pp. 207–218; and V. E. von Gebsattel, "The World of the Compulsive," trans. Sylvia Koppel and Ernest Angel, *Existence*, eds. Rollo May et al. (New York: Basic Books, 1958), pp. 170–187.

[2] Helen Merrell Lynd, *On Shame and the Search for Identity* (New York: Science Editions, 1961).

Finally, depersonalization conveys no moral evaluation. It is a subjective state of being that seems to have consequences for interpersonal relationships. In the case of the police officer, one may well ask how else he is to react to the social environment in which he finds himself. What emerges from my data is that social-structural factors aid, impede, channel, and encourage depersonalized thinking and acting. Depersonalization in RCPD tends not to result from individual choice or proclivity, but, instead, is a response to intolerable conditions established by the community. It is an occupational rather than a moral imperative. Before continuing with the main discussion of this chapter, however, I shall consider this point in terms of the authority-relationships in organizations in general and the defensive bureaucracy of RCPD in particular.

In his interaction with other recruits, academy staff, patrolmen, and administrators, the recruit guides his behavior and is guided by the behavior of others according to their respective status positions. Therefore, a recruit must initiate all salutes to officers or obey orders from any superior regardless of his own feelings in the matter. This is, of course, not unique to police organizations. If any bureaucracy is to operate efficiently, it is necessary for its members to forego personality clashes and to interact on the basis of their respective statuses. Status relationships that are characterized by impersonalism is an organizational goal without which the chances would be slim that organizational output would be efficient.[3] For example, in any subordinate-superordinate relationship, the subordinate is usually more restricted in his action. A worker does not openly defy his foreman, a graduate student does not rebuke his dissertation advisers, nor does the clergyman criticize his hierarchy—unless they are willing to take the possible penalties. The recruit could be dismissed from the academy, the employee fired, the student failed, and the clergyman sent to an isolated community (or if still recalcitrant, excommunicated).

It was mentioned earlier that the character of the police organization may be perceived as a defensive bureaucracy. In some ways the concept of defensive bureaucracy parallels Simmel's concept of the secret society.[4] Secret society members desire autonomy from the characteristics of the larger community. They want privacy, a homoge-

---

[3] Max Weber, *From Max Weber: Essays in Sociology,* edited and translated by H. H. Gerth and C. Wright Mills (New York: Oxford University, 1946), p. 216.

[4] Georg Simmel, *The Sociology of Georg Simmel,* edited and translated by Kurt H. Wolff (New York: Free Press, 1950), pp. 345–376.

nous membership, and personalized relationships. Not finding support from the outer community, they psychologically, emotionally, and intellectually seclude themselves from the outer social environment— no matter how much physical contact they may have. To maintain the norm of secrecy, the organizational structure is centralized. Consequently, the more hostile the social environment is, the more defensive and the more centralized the organization will be.

Although the member of the secret society may find recognition and individuality within the organization, he becomes isolated from the greater community. As the centralized character of a secret society increases, observes Simmel, its members become desocialized (in the sense that the values learned in the organization may conflict with the values of the community) and depersonalized (in the sense that individuality is suppressed for the common good). It is apparent, then, that the strategies used to defend the organization and its members backfire. The same phenomenon that occurs within the secret society also seems to occur within RCPD.

As has been obvious in the last two chapters, the police training program unwittingly (wittingly?) reinforces its own dilemmas. The protective mechanisms employed by police officers individually and collectively against out-group suspiciousness feed out-group suspicions. Also, professionalism seems to have an antiprofessional effect. The same cycle is true regarding depersonalization. The recruit seems to enter the academy with a narrow range of perspectives. The academy tries to broaden his range, but it seems to fall far short of its goals. Indeed, the academy seems to reconfirm the recruit's particularism. Why the academy seemed to fail in this respect and how the recruit seemed to interpret these academy experiences from his narrow cultural ledge is the subject of this chapter.

The issue, then, is not a case of either criticizing or justifying the police structure. The same structure exists elsewhere in our society. The point is, such an arrangement for interaction does exist in fact, and these arrangements have both positive and negative consequences. I am merely trying to discuss one consequence that happened to occur during the training of in-coming police officers in one police department and that happened to be unrecognized by police officers and public alike. Because of the controversial nature of this theme, more reliance will be placed on the actual words of the recruit and his mentors than was done for the other themes.

THE RECRUIT AS DEPERSONALIZED

BY OUT-GROUPS

DIRTY WORK. The public contributes to depersonalization of police officers in several ways—one is by assigning them some of society's dirty work without itself assuming any responsibility for the promotion of law and order under a system of justice.

> Find out how much the citizen wants to be involved. They're always crying the police don't want to do their job, but when you ask them to get involved, then the shoe is on the other foot.

The emotional impact of this on the police officer inclines him to deviate from the rule of due process of law. Lawyers who overlook their social obligations for money and who aid their clients to escape legal sanctions, politicians who sit by smugly as police officers become targets of frustration arising from narrow-minded political promises and decisions, blacks who despise officers merely because they are policemen, newsmen who slant the news against the police for sensational purposes, and the public which sympathizes with a violator if he happens to be injured when he resists arrest, contribute to the depersonalization of the police officer.

Unfortunately, even when he clearly acts outside the due process of law, the officer feels he should not be censured by these groups. Any criticism is antilaw enforcement. Supreme Court decisions that protect the individual from various police practices are also antilaw and order. Press releases of police brutality are automatically biased. When the recruit hears himself and his occupation being disparaged by some of the educated elements of the community, it does not help him to respond objectively to public or legal censure. For example:

R: Sir, I heard a professor at State University say that Rurban County police was where you went if you didn't want to further your education.

I: Now you know why we have such a big problem when an educator says that.

CATEGORIZATION. The police officer is also depersonalized through public stereotyping. The recruit learned early that in joining RCPD he became part of a category. He was stripped of any individuality; no longer would he be perceived as an individual. His actions would reflect on the entire department, perhaps on every officer in the country.

> You are always resented . . . I know if I do something, I can

stereotype the department. . . . If you do something commendable or make a professional or human error, it's "the police," it's not John Jones. You are no longer Bill Brown but Bill Brown, the patrolman.

The recruit and the patrolman apparently perceived the situation accurately, since the public does seem to respond to the police officer as a member of a category. As a black is easily identified as a member of a group by the color of his skin, so the policeman is readily identified by his uniform. Again and again the officer finds himself stereotyped. A news item tells about an ex-policeman who robbed a bank. Although people may think that he has just left the force, further investigation reveals that he has been out of the department for years. As one lecturer put it,

Your conduct off duty—and technically you're never off duty— determines how people judge the police force. Even if you quit, you're branded "ex-cop." Not everyone can get in, but once you're in, you're branded for life.

UNNORMAL RESTRICTIONS. The recruit learned that his newly acquired status did not allow him to engage in behavior in which he might have participated previously in full public view.

You used to have four beers, now you have to have three so you don't stagger. The same people who said, "Look at Joe, he's put one on again, but he deserves it; he works hard," now say "Look at that cop!" You can't engage in loud arguments anymore, even in your own home. They'll say the shield's gone to your head. It doesn't matter that you used to do this all the time.

He also learned that what was previously considered his private business could become public. He was told that if he were to fall behind in his credit, his creditors would complain directly to the commssioner.

As with the clergyman and grade school teacher, the police officer is depersonalized through being granted special considerations by virtue of his status-position, not because of his individual attributes. Furthermore, he is not to engage in social activities open to most other individuals; he is not permitted to be fully human. Niederhoffer relates an attempt by the New York City Police Department to drop an unmarried honor policeman because he was allegedly sleeping with a woman during his probationary period. The department's rationale was that the police must set an example to the citizenry.[5]

---

[5] Arthur Niederhoffer, *Behind the Shield* (Garden City, N.Y.: Doubleday, 1967), p. 109.

No longer may the officer become drunk at parties, no longer may he shout so freely in his own home, no longer is the simple request made of his neighbor to keep his dog from roaming the streets unleashed quite so simple.

The recruit became aware that he was not appreciated for himself but for his occupational status. It became the basis of his total identity and obscured his individuality.

> Once you become a police officer . . . things will change. All
> you'll want is an unlisted phone number. Everybody calls you
> for information. "A new law was passed, what do you think
> about it?" "I have this problem, what do I do?"

Said one recruit in confirmation:

> When you go to a party, you don't want to say you're a cop
> because it seems that they just want to know a cop because
> he's a cop.

The complete unfairness of public categorization was demonstrated to the recruit during a field trip. One of the new courses in the academy curriculum involved visiting State College to acquaint the recruit with police science courses and library facilities available to him after he graduated from the academy. A member of the academy staff happened to be a teacher at State College, and he was asked by the college to wear his uniform for the occasion. Because of his popularity among the recruits, his sense of humor, and his reputation as someone who exemplifies the ideal law enforcer, the recruit class was shocked when he greeted it with the warning:

> I want you to watch yourselves today. I wore this uniform
> for the first time here, and as I walked down the hall, some
> creep called out "paranoid fuck."

BY THE DEPARTMENT

CATEGORIZATION. If the public and out-groups did not treat the police officer as a person with feelings, ideas, prejudices, virtues, and infallibility, neither did the police department. As the department became yet another source of worry to the recruit in his ethos of defensiveness, so it also seemed to contribute to his depersonalization.

One way in which the department appeared to depersonalize its members was to categorize them in the same way that out-groups did. The recruit was taught that the public might categorize and stereotype him, but the instructors themselves seemed to reinforce the recruit's sense of being categorized.

Anything you do that brings discredit to the department,
even *if you are off duty*, is subject to departmental discipline.
[My emphasis]

As a result, the recruit learned that he had to suppress his individuality in order to protect the department from complaints.

AUTHORITY RELATIONSHIPS. In addition to the department's own categorization of its members, the structure and process of academy training seemed to contribute to the recruit's depersonalized feeling. The paramilitary structure dictated that officers interact on the basis of their respective statuses. As Erving Goffman observes, military courtesy gives an officer his due not because of what the subordinates may think of him personally, but in spite of it.[6] "We are quasi-military because if you are told to do something, you do it." Of course, the recruit was constantly aware that he was at the very bottom of the hierarchy. Only with the academy staff did he feel free to speak openly, but this was because the staff made deliberate attempts to establish an atmosphere of trust. Otherwise, if a superior erred or seemed to misjudge a situation, there was little the subordinate could do but "take it" emotionlessly—depersonally. No matter how egalitarian the staff tried to be, one recruit spoke for the rest, "Rank has its privilege." Rank does have its privilege—in RCPD and elsewhere. But in a sense, the subordinate is depersonalized and the superordinate is depersonalizing *if* their interaction is based on their status positions rather than on their individual qualities.

BY OCCUPATIONAL NECESSITY

In many instances the recruit realized he did not dare personalize his relationships. The police officer just cannot afford to differentiate between people: the seasoned criminal and the first offender; the person who challenges a law he believes unjust and the one who acts without regard to ethical considerations. An officer cannot afford to discriminate between people who have different backgrounds, different problems, or different forms of acting out. People are either alive or dead, lawful or criminal, in-group or out-group. He must not

---

[6] Erving Goffman, "The Nature of Deference and Demeanor," *Interaction Ritual* (Chicago: Aldine, 1967), p. 58.

think of the person as an individual human being with a kaleidoscope of expressions, motivations, dreams, and attitudes. Indeed, one of the purposes of police training is to teach in-coming members to enforce the law impartially.

> Now we are only setting up guides. You are going to have to
> make the ultimate decision according to your conscience. Now
> it may be that brain deterioration occurs before the six minutes
> is up [death from asphyxiation is supposed to occur within
> that time], but it is not our decision to decide if he wants to be
> a vegetable or dead. Euthanasia is not our business.

And yet, despite the fact that he frequently must depersonalize, the police officer has considerable discretion over how he handles complaints. Says Thomas Simpson, who teaches at John Jay College of Criminal Justice, "The combination of depersonalization and discretionary power is, for many of my students, a major personal problem in daily life."

PERSONAL JEOPARDY. A film emphasized the personal danger to which an officer exposes himself if he does not rigidly adhere to the "Rules and Procedures" impersonally. The film was entitled "Stay Alert and Live: The Techniques and Mechanics of Arrest." The film showed an officer making an arrest. As he was handcuffing the suspect, he fumbled with the handcuffs and was killed. Another scene showed two plainclothesmen arresting a very meek and mild man for embezzlement at his home. Before they left, he asked if he could pet his cat good-bye. The detectives, touched by his simple request, gave him permission and smiled sympathetically. The suspect came up with a gun, killed the detectives, shot his cat, and then committed suicide. The commentator said at the end of the film:

> Law enforcement officers must be prepared to deal with
> desperate men. These men were even responsible for the
> subject's safety, yet he died, and they died because they were
> careless. You can't let respect, or desire for status, or old
> friendships get in your way. The granting of requests must
> be refused or carefully supervised.

Based on their experiences, the instructors taught that trying to be nice with people was a losing battle; it could only result in trouble. The recruit was admonished never to gamble with people; he was to treat them all on the same level. To do otherwise would not only be unprofessional, it would be dangerous.

> Every incident I know of about a guy who says his wallet is
> at his home and the cop tries to be lenient when a man is close

to his home—I guarantee you'll have trouble. Settle the
situation right away when the incident happens. Don't follow
him home. That's poor procedure. We had two officers injured
when they agreed to follow one guy home, and all his relatives
piled out of the house. It's always the young ones who do it.
If you do it and get away with it, consider yourself lucky.
What if he goes in and doesn't come out? What do you do then?
If you bring them home, you'll wind up using your mace. If you
let him go to his home to get his wallet, you'll wind up rolling
in the grass.

One recruit from Megopolis Department told me a story about an
officer who tried to follow up his "human inclinations." He noticed a
dog had been locked in a car for two days during the hot summer
months. Since it had no food or water, he jimmied the car window
and let it out. "He lost four days vacation. [People] don't want you to
be nice; they don't appreciate it. They don't care about us, so we look
out for ourselves. Fuck 'em."

If the people would allow the officer to be personalizing, claimed
the recruit, he would be. One recruit contended that the difference
between Megopolis Department and RCPD's crime rates was based on
how depersonalizing their respective citizenries were thought to be
toward police officers.

R_1: It's a difference in the people. Look what you get out here:
     mace, nightstick, riot helmet, riot stick, blackjack. They take
     care of you out here. In the city they give you shit. They could
     care less. They don't care about people in the city;
     that's why the crime rates have gone up.

R_2: You can't be nice in the city. If they saw you jacking up a car
     or pushing a civilian's car, they'd ask, "How much are you
     getting?" If you get hurt while pushing a car, you're not
     covered [by workman's compensation], you weren't on duty.
     We're the same. Nick is the same; I'm the same; Fred's the
     same; Vinny's the same. It's the people. In the city they don't
     give a shit about you. Out here, they back you up.

One recruit put it more crudely but succinctly when he compared the
Megopolis City training with Rurban County training. "Well, there's
always a we-they feeling. In the city it was we [and] the public, and
fuck the public. Here it's we [and] the public, serve the public."

It is this sense of alienation from the public that tends to isolate the
officer whose protective stance against out-groups results in a cycle
of distrust between citizen and officer. From the foregoing, one might

assume that in Rurban County the citizen-patrolman relationship is harmonious or that this is discordant with data in previous chapters. Actually, no matter how good police-community relations are, subjectively the citizen is still regarded as a member of an out-group. The dichotomy between "we" and "they" was one way for the recruit to resolve his own ambivalent feelings about the public.

OBJECTIFICATION. Some experiences in the academy had a narcotic effect that encouraged the recruit to perceive people as things. It is quite natural for the police officer to become emotionally involved in a criminal incident with which he comes into contact. Even as a researcher I found myself personally involved in the outcome of two particular crimes. One of the crimes was the murder of a company owner by two robbers when they found out he had no money; the recruit class had been asked to participate in the investigation. The other incident involved what was thought to be a hit-and-run accident at the time; the recruit class had to witness the dead man's autopsy. Until I found out that the murderers were caught and the driver had reported the accident to the police, I was nagged by the worry that both dead men would not have their killers brought to justice. When I admitted my involvement to a patrolman, he replied sympathetically, "That won't last long once you're on the job. [He did not know my research status.] We're working in a rotten world. It gets so you think everyone on the outside is dishonest."

Then, too, the autopsy appeared to be a traumatic experience for everyone. The detachment and delight in their task exhibited by the morticians (probably for the sake of their "audience") offended the recruit and left him with a cold and embittered feeling. Interestingly, in his death the victim was personalized by the recruit the moment the surgical knife sliced through his body.

Man, it sure makes me feel less human after seeing that— just cut up.

Well, as long as you believe in reincarnation, I suppose it's okay. If you believe in Christ, he can do it again.

Hey, does anybody know a religion where you're not allowed to have an autopsy? My wife wants to join one where it's against the religion. . . . If I ever saw a doctor giving an autopsy to a baby, I think I'd take my gun and kill him.

I got a feeling of "so what?" Here's a guy who didn't do anything, just got hit by a car, and they chop you up. It makes you wonder if it's all worth it. Why bother to live.

To protect himself from becoming similarly involved with a victim again, the recruit learned to perceive the individual as an object. The following discussion ensued after a particularly grisly film (which recorded actual highway accidents) was shown to the class.

R₁: Don't you think that guy [the instructor] is dead?

R₂, R₃: Yeah, he's a loser all the way.

RH: He's pretty intense about it all, but if I had to see every day what I saw in the film, I'd be pretty emotional about it too.

R₃: Don't you think he's self-righteous? Soon as he said he didn't drink, I said, "Oh, boy." That wasn't called for.

R₄: (to RH) No, you have to laugh it off.

RH: Laugh it off?

R₄: Sure, you have to laugh at it or you'd go crazy. That's the only way. You have to laugh and say, "You deserve it, you son of a bitch, driving like that."

RH: What about the innocent parties?

R₄: You can't think about it. You can't.

It may be argued that this situational depersonalization permits the officer to continue to fulfill his tasks efficiently or to continue personalizing in other situations. The point here, however, is its overall contribution to what I call recruit depersonalization. Once the recruit learns that he is depersonalized by the public and by his own department and that he must be depersonalizing through occupational necessity, the stage is set for him to depersonalize others.

THE RECRUIT AS DEPERSONALIZING

The focus of this chapter is not on which came first: public depersonalization or police depersonalization, public suspicion and hostility or police suspicion and hostility. But what is important to understand is the process of depersonalization, because until there is mutual understanding, there is no communication or resolution of problems. Some recruits and police officers are sure to object to the term depersonalization. They would prefer the term "impersonal" and, in part, they are correct. However, I am trying to reach the psychological

dimensions that go beyond the occupationally necessary impersonalization and "objectivity" that are recognized and intended by police
officers. It is important to emphasize that there can be a depersonal
quality of interaction *whether or not* the relationship is based on
personalism or impersonalism! Ultimately, an impersonal perspective
combined with hyperdefensiveness takes its toll on the emotional well-
being of the officer. It is this facet that is largely unrecognized and
ignored.

For instance, what is the reaction of a police officer who finds that
good intentions, hard work, dedication, and justice may count for
nothing in a court of law because of a technicality—such as the wrong
person signing a complaint? What is the reaction of an officer when,
in the event physical violence is necessary to effect an arrest, a news
release results in public sympathy with the violator even if he seriously injured an officer in the scuffle? Both of these incidents were
related to me during Field Week, and I have no reason to doubt that
other recruits heard similar stories. It is the long-term effect of these
incidents, and others like them which occur over and over again,
that is important to understand. It is all the more important when it is
recognized that predispositions toward depersonalization are learned
and reinforced in academy training. Indeed, the police are not alone
in this natural response to the kinds of situations in which the officer
finds himself. Parallel processes may be observed among social workers, doctors, lawyers, judges, politicians, psychiatrists, educators,
carpenters, and mechanics.

CATEGORIZATION

DICHOTOMIES. Finding himself depersonalized, the recruit depersonalizes in return. As he is categorized, so he categorizes others. For all
practical purposes, each group is dichotomized into a law-abiding
police supportive group and a criminal antipolice group without
regard for the many other dimensions that make up a person. Thus,
students who demonstrate are "bad," and students who want to go to
classes are "good," and liberal politicians are "bad," and conservative
politicians are "good." A statement made by an officer during the
field trip at State College offered another example of this tendency
toward dichotomizing.

We will be divided up into small groups after the initial
orientation. The boys who will be guiding us think like we do.

> They are police science majors with intentions of joining the
> police force, so don't confuse them with the others.

What this officer seemed to be saying was that the recruit should
define police science students differently from "the others." The
former's potential in-group status apparently determined their worth.
The remark suggested that students who held beliefs different from
those of the recruit were in some undefined way morally inferior or
substandard.

Those persons who supported the police were also depersonalized,
since they seemed to be accepted by the recruit merely on the basis
of that support. All other considerations seemed to be waved aside.
A judge was evaluated in terms of whether or not he punished those
persons brought to trial. Whether he was just or unjust, enlightened or
prejudiced, compassionate or sadistic were facts not sought. Likewise,
said one recruit regarding a popular television personality, "Hey,
Allen Burke loves cops ... ! Yeah, he's a cop lover. He never opens
his mouth when he has a cop on."

There seemed to be little sensitivity to or regard for situational
factors by either the recruit or his instructors. Such factors would
include whether a person was a criminal or a nonconformist, whether
the law in question was just or unjust,[7] whether the law enforced
private morality or public morality,[8] what were the motivations of the
violator, and whether the definition of the situation by the officer himself was self-righteous or unprejudiced. About the only factors that
seemed significant to the officer were the violator's age, class membership, appearance, degree of respect for the officer and the law, and
whether a law was actually violated.

The police officer, in turn, would be quite correct to claim that it is
his duty to arrest anybody he observes who breaks a law. Indeed, he
would be committing a crime himself if he did not arrest a person who
was committing a crime or if he tried to apply some of the above
considerations to the problem at hand. In addition, the officer would
probably argue, if the considerations were applied, they would reinforce favoritism when enforcing the law.

And so they would. It is the court that must make these kinds of
decisions according to the American legal structure. But two qualifica-

---

[7] For a discussion of the criteria for "just laws," see Lon L. Fuller, *The Morality of Law*
(New Haven: Yale University, 1964).

[8] See H. L. A. Hart, *Law, Liberty, and Morality* (New York: Vintage Books, 1963).

tions must be made in this regard. First, it is well-known that the police officer does make decisions of this type every day: which of the laws he simply cannot bother to enforce; if five or ten miles over the speed limit is permissible; who will get a warning, who will be given a summons, and who will be brought to the precinct house for a formal arrest.[9] He decides to be harsher with those who are unconventionally dressed; he may apply some laws to "long-hairs" which he would not apply to more conventionally attired persons. As one recruit remarked to me, "When I catch a long-hair, I don't give him a break."

Second, this attitude still reflects the process of depersonalization. Patrolmen and recruits alike claim their job is to enforce law, not to interpret it. As professionals, they must be impersonal. "There may be validity to the man's excuse, but that's not our job. We don't judge. All we do is present the facts."

However, as noted above, the police officer invokes informal justice every day. Not to become involved in one way or another would be impossible. Furthermore, the recruit's attitudes seemed quite clear each time he heard of a "liberal" Supreme Court decision or of a case dismissed by County Court. In the words of one recruit, "One thing I disagree with is not letting it bother you when a guy walks out of jail when you arrest him. If you take your job seriously, it's got to bother you."

INTOLERANCE. Again and again the recruit demonstrated a dichotomizing and depersonalizing attitude toward various groups. People were either law-abiding or not. Radical students were spoiled. Liberal politicians were subversive. Blacks were criminally inclined. Intentions had no place in law enforcement, especially if the person belonged to a major out-group. After an announcement that several students who staged a sit-in at State University had been sentenced to 15 days in jail, the recruits were joyous. Although much of their pleasure probably lay in the relief of knowing that students who seemed to break the law intentionally and with impunity had finally

---

[9] Howard S. Becker, *The Outsiders* (New York: Free Press, 1963), pp. 158–162; Jerome H. Skolnick and J. Richard Woodworth, "Bureaucracy, Information, and Social Control," pp. 99–136, and Carl Werthman and Irving Piliavin, "Gang Members and the Police," pp. 56–98, both in *The Police* (New York, John Wiley, 1966); and Irving Piliavin and Scott Briar, "Police Encounters with Juveniles," *American Journal of Sociology*, 70 (Sept. 1964), pp. 209–211.

been convicted, absolutely no concern was directed toward the motivations of the sit-in students. Perhaps the recruits assumed that the sit-in was aimed only at disrupting campus life and involved persons who felt exempted from the law. In any case, the perspective was depersonalizing. The law was broken and that was all that mattered. The victory was twice as delicious since it involved "spoiled" and "disrespectful" youth.

Homosexuals and marijuana smokers seemed to be other targets of recruit depersonalization. Homosexuals were thought to be degenerate both morally and sexually. The recruit could not understand why these degenerates should have the same privileges under the law as respectable people had. The Mattachine Society was condemned for their articles explaining the rights of the homosexual if he were arrested. One instructor referred disgustedly to the legal protection afforded to homosexuals (such as the right to congregate together) as if it were as incredible as the idea that they could possibly lead socially and economically productive lives.

> We used to knock out 150 homosexual places a year in Megopolis
> City. We don't send police academy graduates to these places
> anymore. Majority opinion under [Chief Justice] said, "So let
> them dance!"

The most powerful impact on the recruit regarding sexual deviants occurred during a film made by an out-of-state police agency. It was taken by a hidden camera in a public men's room where homosexuals were known to congregate.[10] The purpose of the film was to show how to identify persons who engaged in sexual aberrations (the acts most frequently shown were oral and anal sodomy) in order to construct a file of suspects for any child molesting complaints that might occur in the future.

The film opened with a scene of several men dragging a lake. The narrator explained, "Are these men searching for evidence to convict a murderer? No, worse. They are looking for evidence to convict a child molester." The battered bodies of two little girls who had refused to engage in oral sodomy were shown. The narrator continued, "Some people would have us not prosecute until they murder or maim

---

[10] For an inside study of homosexual activities in public places, see Laud Humphreys, "Tearoom Trade: Impersonal Sex in Public Places," *Trans-Action*, 7 (January 1970), pp. 10–25. There is a rumor among sociologists that the FBI is presently using this study to imply that Humphreys is a homosexual himself because of his role in campus demonstrations.

people. The violations are unnatural and immoral." At the end of the film, the two beaten bodies were again shown followed by photographs of their smiling faces when they were alive. The narrator closed with the words, "Sex perverts are thought of as harmful only to themselves, but all too often they seek others and eventually seek a younger and younger victim." When some of the recruits laughed at the acts between the men in the film, the instructor admonished them sharply. "Don't laugh at this. These are the people the courts keep letting go. They are murderers."

The message of both the film and the instructor was that homosexuals conformed to a law against nature which dictated that they would turn to younger and younger subjects on whom to foist their degeneracy. Therefore, it would be best to permanently lock up these people on their first offense, since they eventually would turn to child molesting. Techniques such as hidden cameras in public rest rooms could be used to identify these perverts. Evidence contradicting the "child molester" assumption, the identification of homosexual with child molester, and the fact that many confirmed homosexuals can and do lead very productive lives, was never touched on.

Marijuana smokers and drug addicts suffered from similar categorical perceptions by the recruit and his instructors. Through a series of vivid films and lectures, the initial prejudices of the recruit were reconfirmed and increased. By the end of the lessons, the recruit was particularly intolerant toward persons who continued to break the laws governing marijuana and drug use—especially students, hippies, or people who sold marijuana to public school children. He seemed very concerned and angered when an instructor noted that Megopolis City expected 1500 deaths among school-age children from overdoses of drugs.

Unfortunately, the lectures and films were designed to appeal to the emotions of the recruit rather than to his reason. For instance, no mention was made of the medical knowledge regarding marijuana. Neither was there any discussion of the more enlightened and promising drug treatment experiments that have largely been condemned by national, state, and local narcotics agencies.[11] The recruit learned his lessons well, since they apparently fed the beliefs he had had in the first place. Marijuana should be illegal because, the recruit parrots his

---

[11] Edwin M. Schur, *Our Criminal Society* (Englewood Cliffs, N.J.: Prentice-Hall, 1969), pp. 213–219.

instructors, everyone who is on heroin started with marijuana. And, "When you drink too much, you fall asleep; when you have too much marijuana, you can rape someone and never even remember it." Because of emotionally loaded statements like these, and the fact that evidence contradicting this point of view was never presented, the recruit was not really well-informed on the subject of marijuana, in particular, and drugs, in general. Consequently, his attitude was biased and overemotional.

For instance, the day of our exposure to an autopsy, the body of an eighteen-year-old boy who died from an overdose of heroin was wheeled out of the "freezer" for his mother to identify and claim. Still shaky from the grisly experience of a few moments ago, we felt that drugs such as marijuana must be wiped out completely by any means possible when we saw the youth who had suffered the same indignities as the man who had been "butchered" in the next room. But of particular interest was the fact that, in contrast to the recruits' personalization of the old man in his death, they depersonalized this youngster. Perhaps the rigid stance they took in the following conversation reflected their desire to never again become emotionally involved in the face of personal tragedy.

R_1:   How old is he?

R_2:   Eighteen.

R_1:   Christ! Well, if he lived, he'd be stealing from someone.

R_2:   Yeah, we'd just have to do it later in his life.

R_3:   The bastard got what he deserved.

RH: Maybe he didn't know how much he was taking.

R_1, R_2, R_3, R_4: So what? Would you put a gun to your head and pull the trigger? He was an addict—it's better for everybody all around.

Still another example illustrates the recruit's tendency to depersonalize. I testily asked one recruit what he would do with a supposedly peaceful demonstration if the participants refused to disperse on an order by the police.

R: Take them away.

RH: How?

R: Like this. [He demonstrates a come-along hold on me.]

RH: What if they still don't go? Wouldn't sticks be better?
After all, that might encourage the others to move.

R: No, you don't have to use nightsticks. One reason is you get
time-and-a-half, and besides, you have to make out a report
on every person you hit.

For this recruit, a rough treatment of peaceful protesters should not
be used because of the paper work involved and because the longer
it took to disperse them, the more overtime he would get. The fact that
the protesters were nonviolent was not significant.

In spite of his apparent depersonalizing tendencies, this recruit
seemed to believe that in the long run he would enforce the law more
justly—indeed, more humanely—than do judges and lawyers. He
believed that the recent rulings of the Supreme Court ignored the
right of the victim to have his assailant punished. When lawyers win
their cases on technicalities and when judges provide them with the
opportunities, they are the ones who are inhumane and depersonal.

It used to be that if a woman screamed "thief" and you saw the
thief, you could run after him, bring him in front of the woman,
and ask if he's the one who did it. If she said no, you let him go;
if she said yes, you locked him up.

Now you remember the doctor and his wife who were shot
during a robbery. He entered the home, stole what he wanted.
He shot the husband in the head and killed him; he shot the wife
in the head, also a physician, and she lived. We caught the
perpetrator, brought him to her bedside in the hospital where
she said, "Yes, he's the one who killed my husband and shot me."
He was tried and convicted. The Supreme Court said, "No, we are
setting up guidelines; the victim and suspect cannot meet until
trial." The gun and the brain are no longer guidelines; you have
to be a lawyer, judge, and counselor.

Such a disparity of justice as perceived by the police officer may be
one important reason why he appears to be rigid and self-righteous
when he catches a speeding motorist, a demonstrating youth, or a
thief: the violator represents *all* those who got away.

The recruit did believe that the laws should be applied equally to
the entire citizenry. But when one is a sex pervert, a murderer, or a
drunk, he becomes less equal ipso facto. The student who flouts con-
ventional morality and the black who is a member of a group that has
a statistically high crime rate are less equal, since their membership
category indicates that they are more likely to break a law than are
members of other groups. All people are equal under the law to begin

with, but their appearance, demeanor, and attitudes qualify their state
of equality.

UNNORMAL PRIVILEGES. Previously it was shown how the recruit
found himself depersonalized by out-group members because of his
occupational status. In that connection, some illustrations were given
regarding the restrictions placed on him, on- and off-duty. In turn, the
recruit depersonalizes others by categorizing them and by expecting
preferential treatment on the basis of his uniform. Obtaining services
"on the arm" was discussed as a part of the ethic of cutting corners
in an earlier chapter. However, the officer's status affects his day-to-
day relationships in another way.

The police officer interacts with the citizen on the basis of power and
status, always aware of the potential threat that he wields over the
citizen. Power becomes an important component of the patrolman's
working personality and his relationships. When some members of the
Traffic Squad (the only group on the force who wear Gestapo-type
trousers and leather jackets) came to the academy for in-service training, the recruits were told by a staff member, "dressed as they are,
they're psychologically set to command a situation." The regular uniform seemed to have a similar, if lower-keyed, effect on the recruit.

A couple of anecdotes from Field Week indicate the recruit's con-
sciousness of the nature of his relationships. One *jokingly* admitted a
sense of power as he directed traffic: "I loved to point to the guy and
direct him to turn; I loved it." Another recruit experienced his power
in a direct face-to-face confrontation.

> We went on a family disturbance call. My partner said I should
> try handling it, but he was right behind me. There was this drunk
> who said he wanted to go to jail: "My wife says I'm drunk, and
> I want to go to jail." I told him, "You only go to jail if you're under
> arrest, and if I put you under arrest, you won't be coming back!"
> "No, no, I don't want to go to jail." "Sit down," I told him. I felt
> in control of the situation. Power! Of course [he added
> humorously], uh, my partner was right behind me all the time.

For these two recruits, at least, power relationships became an important component of interaction. This by no means is to imply that the
recruit learns to abuse his authority, but shows he was aware that;
in the last analysis, individual qualities were subordinate to the relative status positions between the actors.

An experience of my own was both passive and amusing. I was
dressed in full uniform on a highway waiting for a friend to pick
me up. While I was waiting, a businessman who was leaving his work

for the day started to drive from his parking lot entrance into the flow of traffic. When he noticed my uniform and my riot stick, which was sticking out of a snowbank, he stopped, turned around after an exerting series of maneuvers, threw a few resentful glances toward me, and drove to the exit lane. Although I did not care which lane he used, my presence alone determined his actions, and I felt a sense of pride and self-righteousness.

It would seem, then, that the recruit enjoys certain privileges by virtue of his uniform which he would probably be hesitant to surrender. On the surface, this would seem to contradict the recruit's apparent resentment over the public's stereotyping of him. In clearing up this contradiction, it may be that the recruit *does* agree to being stereotyped. What he takes exception to is not the stereotyping itself, but the content of the stereotype: he is stereotyped incorrectly.[12] The recruit may even concede that some negative parts of the stereotype are correct although, he would say, they apply less to his department, or to himself. The recruit seems to want to be stereotyped—but in accordance with the professional image that he has of himself, of his department, and of his occupation.

COPS AND ROBBERS

The final examples of recruit training as depersonalizing stem from recruit conversations about youthful peccadillos. In this particular recruit class, 29 percent of the recruits were in police records for either questioning, an arrest, or a conviction. Only a guess can be made as to how representative this was of the rest of the class, which did not come to the official attention of the police. Whatever the case, the discussions reflected that the typical recruit engaged in some form of "deviant" behavior that could have ended in an arrest before he joined the department. The class was amused, for instance, when an instructor, recognizing a recruit during his lecture, clasped his hands:

Oh, my God, McVey! I'd like a nickel for every time I chased him over the fence. (Laughter) Now he's a cop! You were a lousy bastard. (Laughter) Remember when I was a rookie and you threw an egg at my wife? (Laughter)

Another recruit confided to me that he had been in trouble when he

---

[12] I thank Natalie Allon for this observation.

had been a member of a gang. He referred to an officer who had known him during those years.

> That sergeant is in the third precinct, and I've seen him a couple of times. He looks at me as if he can't quite place me, and I hope he never does. God, I hope I'm not assigned to the third. If he recognizes me, I'll probably get thrown out of here.

In fact, the department did have a record of him on file, and he was not "thrown out of here."

Most of the accounts discussed in which a recruit came up against the police stemmed from drag racing or speeding. Some recruits related experiences in which they had escaped police pursuit. Two of them excited their fellow recruits by describing accidents that resulted from their speeding. In both examples, the car was demolished and the recruit was nearly killed. Also, the accidents occurred only after skillful maneuvering to avoid crashing into another car or to avoid hitting a pedestrian. Both stories were told proudly and were received respectfully. After the discussion, I exclaimed,

RH: Jesus Christ! I think all you guys were hell-raisers somewhere along the line.

R: Well, we can understand them because we experienced it.

It may seem odd that these "hell-raisers" would join an occupation that tries to prevent the same kind of behavior in which they used to engage. Actually, it is not as surprising as one might think. The focal concerns which, according to Walter Miller, are esteemed by lower-class delinquents are also the values that are necessary to perform police work: trouble, toughness, excitement, smartness, autonomy, and fatalism. Police work is exciting, fun, and dangerous; it involves both an ideology of heroism and qualities of manhood. I myself became more acceptable to several recruits when I admitted that I had been on disciplinary probation as an undergraduate: "Sure, he's a regular guy . . . everybody's got to get in trouble at least once."

The recruit was still playing cops and robbers; all that he had done was to switch roles. Whereas at one time he was an antiestablishment rebel, now he was the establishment itself. He still looked forward to the thrill of the high-speed chase, but now he was the chaser. The recruit was warned time and time again by staff members, who apparently were aware of the recruit's tendency to speed with the siren blasting, that he must slow down at intersections; it was more important to reach the scene of a call than to become a call oneself. Nevertheless, one instructor sadly admitted to the class:

You're going to get a taut feeling in your stomach on the chase. By God, I know I felt my heart pumping with excitement, but if I crossed that intersection like he did—without regard for traffic— there would have been a total [damage to the car]. All that you learn here will go out the window as that adrenaline goes through you.

However, instead of understanding speeders "because we experienced it," the recruit reacted self-righteously during and after the chase (I did in my chase, too). The attempted escape was looked forward to as a duel between two competitors, but it also seemed to be an affront to his authority. For instance, after Field Week, midway through the training period, the recruits shared their experiences with the staff. One of them had been in the most exciting chase of the week, which some of us had heard over car radios.

R: We had a high speed chase.

S: How did you feel through it all?

R: Well, my partner was a bit angry.

S: That's a natural reaction.

R: We did a job on the driver. (Laughter) He was kicking all the time and resisted handcuffing. It's good to see how a prisoner struggles all the way, after academy training.

S: How did the fight happen?

R: He knew what was going to happen.

S: He knew he was going to get it, so he decided to get his licks in first?

According to this recruit, it was a foregone conclusion that the speeder was going to get some "justice without trial" once he was captured. Thus the recruit, who in his youth might have met the police head-on, had joined a social control agency and sometimes reacted self-righteously toward the deviation of others.

Nowhere was this more apparent than in his intolerance of the political dissident and the student protester. The protester and the student present problems to the police that differ from the usual cop and robber interaction because they do not subscribe to the values that seem to be held by both the police officer and the robber. The "robber" believes in the legitimacy of the laws; he breaks the law without fanfare and without appeal to a higher morality. His capture is perceived by the police officer as a challenge between two clever protagonists. Both cop and robber are in a competitive game in which one wins by outwitting the other. Finally, the robber's capture is rewarded by public praise.

In contrast, the dissident and protester challenge the existing authorities. They break laws for an ethical cause, and they may actively seek publicity. There is no challenge to their capture, since they may willingly remain for and submit to arrest. And their arrest is just as likely to provoke public wrath as it is to stimulate public appreciation.

In the case of the student protester (who is also likely to be a political dissident), the problem is much more ideological. That is, the student is castigated more for his general life-style than for any specific act such as a sit-down strike. In part, the problem lies in the authority-control issue. The student seems to be competing for authority with the police officer; he is in favor of more individualized and less standardized authority, which to the recruit represented no authority at all. The student was castigated by the recruit for his sexual permissiveness and apparent disrespect for the law. Yet probably a streak of envy on the recruit's part was involved, since stories of sexual exploits and youthful peccadillos were plentiful among the recruits. In one discussion this envy became manifest.

R_1: Hey, are there a lot of girls in ——?

RH: Oh, sure. There's . . . .

R_1: (interrupting) Yeah, but do they fuck?

RH: Sure.

R_1: I don't believe in that shit.

R_2: Yeah, that's going kind of far.

RH: I don't mind it.

R_2: That's our middle-class values, I guess. (Pauses)
    I wish it happened when I was in college.

RH: (laughing) *Now* he comes out with it.

R_1: It's not right. What if it's your sister—or your daughter!

R_2: Listen to him, the biggest scumbag of them all.

The antagonism against the student seemed to be exacerbated by the recruit's background. The typical recruit had come from a "working class" family, struggled through high school, fulfilled his military obligation, and worked on several jobs before joining RCPD. Whatever he had or had not become, he had accomplished on his own, without parental help. For the recruit, law enforcement in RCPD represented a noble service, economic success, a step upward in status, and full "middle class" membership. But in the recruit's struggle for upward mobility, he saw that the educated "middle class" youth was rejecting the values of his parents, which were the recruit's own values.

To have worked to reach the symbols of success only to find them in the process of revision on arrival had two detrimental consequences for the recruit. It resulted in an entrenchment behind the status quo, since he was unwilling to accept change now that he had "made it." Indeed, with more and more clergymen becoming political and social activists, the police occupation may have been perceived as the last firm buttress of the crumbling middle-class morality. It also resulted in a rejection of and intolerance for unconventional attitudes and behavior, which the recruit defined as immoral because they represented threats to society's integrity. Consequently, those youths who wore long hair and unconventional apparel, challenged traditional sex roles, smoked marijuana, lived in communes, or demonstrated against forms of authority (police, university administration, and national government) were morally inferior persons, regardless of their education or intentions.

Erik Erikson, who related Freudian psychology to society, observes that autonomy-control, a stage in personality development, revolves around "holding on" and "letting go." Each mode can lead to either benign or hostile expectations and attitudes. The "hold" may be a dictatorial restraint or a pattern of care; the "letting go" may be of destructive forces or of a relaxed letting pass.[13] A basic problem of police action today seems to be knowing when to hold on or let go, to restrain or to care for, to unleash punitive forces or to let be.

Instead of allowing variations in behavior to "pass by" if they do not (1) involve direct physical force, (2) exploit minors or other vulnerable persons, or (3) present clear threats to public order and decency, law enforcers demand more repressive laws, for example, to combat the threat of political dissident and student protester

---

[13] Erik H. Erikson, *Childhood and Society* (New York: W. W. Norton, 1963), 2nd ed., p. 251; and "Identity and the Life Cycle," *Psychological Issues*, 1 (1959), pp. 65–74.

ideologies.[14] Tougher laws, not a more rational system of laws and their enforcement, are perceived as solutions to the problems of private morality, conceptions of bad taste, and political orthodoxy.

THE POLICE ACADEMY AND FALSE PERSONALIZATION[15]

Based on my observations in the police academy, depersonalization seems to have four basic components. One is the tendency to categorize or stereotype others instead of perceiving them as individuals. As stereotyped, they are perceived as devoid of human characteristics; they are objectified. Secondly, depersonalization is characterized by relationships that are based on respective statuses instead of individual merits. Status relationships involve restrictions such as not becoming drunk, obligations such as obeying any and all commands from a superior, and privileges such as free coffee or movies. Since the relationships are based on statuses, this leads to categorizing and deindividualizing. The third component of depersonalization is the tendency to dichotomize people, ideas, and things without appreciation for their nuances. Finally, depersonalization involves an insensitivity to and intolerance for attitudes and behavior that differ from one's own. These components not only underlie depersonal interaction but also provide a basis for judging oneself and others.

In this last section of the chapter I discuss those academy classes that I believe were intended to counter the recruit's tendency to depersonalize by broadening his perspective. These classes include community relations, role playing, self-defense, first aid, justification for the use of force, civil guarantees, and civil disorders. Generally, it seemed that they, in fact, either *reinforced* or were neutralized by the tendencies toward depersonalization. Only the last three classes

---

[14] These are the three criteria which a body of legal experts believe should be used for invoking any criminal law. Those laws which do not conform to these guidelines should be stricken. See Report of the Committee on Homosexual Offenses and Prostitution, *The Wolfenden Report* (New York: Lancer Books, 1964), pp. 20–21. See also Edwin M. Schur, *Our Criminal Society*, for major consequences of suppressing behavioral variations through criminal legislation.

[15] The phrase "false personalization" is taken from David Riesman et al., who used it to refer to the manipulation of people by trying to be personalizing toward them. *The Lonely Crowd* (New Haven: Yale University, 1961), pp. 126–140 and 261–285.

seemed to be somewhat beneficial, but even in them the instructors were unable to draw out and discuss the attitudes of the recruit effectively. Of course, some instructors whose courses were not specifically geared to counteract depersonalization made open-minded and liberal statements, but here, too, there were limitations. These statements were generally isolated comments made with little or no explanation, and either drowned in the elaborate and plentiful comments of other instructors or were neutralized by the lecturer's own side comments.

For example, several instructors pointed out that the recent Supreme Court decisions were not objectionable to an officer who performed his job professionally anyway. But that was as far as they would go. Never did an instructor delve into *why* the recruit should not define the Court's decisions as antilaw enforcement. Since a substantial number of other instructors made thorough explanations about why the decisions were, in fact, antilaw enforcement, and since the recruit was probably disposed against the rulings initially, mere one-sentence comments to the contrary (for example, "Then we got the Miranda warning that set back law enforcement ten years—*if* you look at it from an antiquated view; but from an experienced view, it's not so bad as you might think") could not have had much of a countering effect on the recruit.

Two instructors referred to the Chicago police riot during the 1968 Democratic National Convention in lectures designed to impress on the recruit the need to enforce the law fairly. The message that seemed to come across to the recruit, however, was that the "real" crime of the police riot was not in the totalitarian atmosphere of the convention, or in the intolerance toward the ideas of the young (ideas that were borne out in the top secret *Pentagon Papers*, illegally published in the summer of 1971), or in the brutality and sadism by which a substantial number of officers (although a minority) "maintained order." The real crime was that it "didn't look good for law enforcement."

> I'm not a liberal and don't sympathize with ultra-liberals. But as an objective person, I can say if a policeman or a citizen was in error. If a bag of ——— is thrown at me, does it give me a right to bang fourteen heads where the bag came from and they didn't even do it? [Some recruits whisper yes] There is much evidence that the police over-reacted in Chicago. It doesn't follow reasonably. *They had something coming, those weirdos.* But does this give us a right to disgrace ourselves by sinking to their level? [My emphasis]
> ... What we have to do is approach these situations with

reason. If the Democratic Convention with 10,000 hippies comes
here in four years, I don't want *Life* to be able to criticize us.

Earlier in the training session, slides that were taken during the
Chicago riot were shown to the recruits in a lecture that depicted the
various kinds of individuals with which an officer might come into
contact: the angry, the frightened, the desperate, the drunk, the
ashamed, and the criminal. The gist of the lecture was that each type
of individual had to be handled in a different way. The instructor
closed his lecture saying, "A police officer must enforce *all* the laws
according to the County Charter," and he showed two slides. Slide A
was a picture of a group of demonstrators apparently facing a police
cordon; one of them in the forefront angrily had his middle finger
extended. The other slide, slide B, showed a burly sergeant with his
riot stick raised high above his head.

If a man acts like this [shows slide A], don't react like this
[shows slide B]. It's a hell of a weapon to use against us. You
know what he deserves [shows slide A] and may be thrilled at
[shows slide B] this. (Laughter)

These instructors seemed to believe that the demonstrators "got
what they deserved," even though up to a third of the on-duty Chicago
police ruined the professional image for law enforcers in general.
The recruits apparently agreed with them. As they filed out of the
classroom, I overheard the comments: "...beat their faces right in,"
"let 'em shove you, then crown 'em," "I'd hit the first long-hair that
got within range."

The treatment of the Chicago riot was not the only example in
which the consideration of other people's individuality as an end in
itself was ignored for more "manipulative" ends. Maintaining good
police-community relations was one of them: "Believe me, this is how
we get our money; this is how it's done." Another reason given for why
an officer should not depersonalize people was his inability to know
with whom he was dealing or who might be watching him: "Be
courteous because you don't know who you're talking to."

A few instructors encouraged the recruit to show more understanding beyond just "getting the job done." Being able to communicate
with people was a necessary skill in police work.

Unreasonable noise is disorderly conduct. If you receive a call,
technically you can arrest him. If you have to arrest everyone
you come to, you're not a "hot cop," you don't know people.
You've got to learn how to con and communicate. If you can't
communicate, you're in the wrong business.

The recruit was told to try to educate the public, since people were not aware of all the laws in the books. "Pull them over and explain the law; people expect you to show some understanding."

If the people became too well-versed in the law, however, it could cause the police officer a great deal of aggravation when he interacted with them in an official capacity. For instance, an instructor held up an *Ebony* magazine in front of the class.

> This book in particular, you see the sub-title, "What to do if
> Arrested?" At first glance this looks a little anti-police. That's
> all we need is more sharp men telling us what to do. Here they
> set down the "do's" and "dont's" in a way the layman can
> understand. Our job is never that easy: we have to use discretion
> and intelligence. Now this is what is happening. In some cases
> they can tell you what their rights are and what your rights
> are. So look it up and read it. It can be enlightening for you.
> See what they're learning on the outside.

Later in the day, I leafed through the magazine article with another recruit.

RH: This doesn't seem anti-police. It's just telling them just about what we were told to adhere to while making arrests.

R: That's one side.

RH: You mean now they can tell the cop what to do?

R: Yes.

RH: Aren't you supposed to educate the public?

R: From our view it hinders law enforcement.

RH: What if it happened to you?

R: Then it's me.

RH: Are you serious?

R: Sure.

If the average citizen knew his rights completely, one of the advantages of the patrolman during an altercation would be lost. Unfortunately, the defensive ethos among police officers pits the people against the police. Unfortunately, too, the public seems to make this posture necessary. The more knowledge the people have, the more ability they have to challenge the authority of the officer. As Fisher observes, when a group is challenged by its clientele, it may depart from efforts to educate them and attempt to discredit their motives or the accuracy of their knowledge.[16] Conning replaces meaningful communication. One communicates not to develop mutual understanding, but to make the job easier.[17]

Apparently aware of the ambivalent feelings of police officers in their dealings with the public, the staff included classes within the curriculum that were designed to foster a more personalizing attitude. But in the last analysis, it was depersonalization that seemed to be fostered. It is these classes that I now consider.

OBJECTIFICATION: SELF-DEFENSE AND FIRST AID

The lessons in self-defense, karate, come-along techniques, and the use of night and riot sticks reinforced the tendency of the recruits and patrolmen to "objectify" individuals. That is, the lessons seemed to encourage the recruit to perceive an opponent as a "thing." Again I emphasize that the purpose at this point in the discussion, as in the entire chapter, is not to deal with the question: "What else can an officer do when physical force is required or if he is threatened with bodily harm?" Of course, the officer cannot be expected to look on his opponent as misunderstood by his family or in need of a doctor's care. Instead, the purpose is to try to describe and understand one process among several that seemed to occur during the police training program.

In some ways the staff was successful in its effort to encourage personalization. For example, the initial step suggested in riot control was to permit the attacking person alternative lines of action: of retreating or of continuing the attack. The purpose was to provide the attacker or demonstrator with a choice so that he would not jump to the conclusion that his only line of action was to defend himself by attacking. "You don't surround them like they did in Frisco and Chicago and then order them to disperse. Leave them a path out."

One way of providing a demonstrator with a choice is to hold a

---

[16] Bernice M. Fisher, "Claims and Credibility: A Discussion of Occupational Identity and the Agent-Client Relationship," *Social Problems,* 16 (Spring 1969), pp. 423–433.

[17] For a good description of the conning techniques used by the patrolman, see H. Taylor Buckner, "The Police: The Culture of a Social Control Agency" (unpublished Ph.D. dissertation), University of California at Berkeley, Department of Sociology, 1967.

riot stick in both hands as if it were a cue stick used in a game of pool, so that it can be pushed forward and back in pulsating movements through the lead hand. The first spar is directed toward the face, but it is a warning movement only. No contact is made unless the demonstrator decides to run into the butt himself or to stand his ground. This pulsating movement to the face continues as long as the demonstrator moves back. If he stands his ground or attacks, the first *intended* contacting thrust would be to a part of the torso. The purpose of these tactics was not only to provide the attacker with a few more seconds to reconsider his choice of action without being struck but also to give the officer a chance to find out if the demonstrator wished to retreat. Neither opponent sees the other as posing only one line of action for him if this procedure is followed. During a sit-in at State University, the students were offered several alternatives that resulted in the orderly arrest of 15 extremists and earned RCPD a great deal of praise from the community. The Chicago police offered only one line of action with disastrous results.

Generally, however, training methods seemed to objectify both the recruit and the opponent. The recruits were taught karate movements "so it will be as instinctive to you later as it is now to duck objects." Defensive techniques were taught with little regard for the opponent. As a threat, he must be dealt with efficiently and practically. The directions included the following:

> . . . hit the man with only the first two knuckles so all the force
> is concentrated in a small area; don't hit with your wrist bent,
> hit straight at the man keeping your other hand close to your
> body with the knuckles up—if you don't, you lose your force
> because there is give in your wrists; don't hit with your fingers,
> or you'll break them; hit straight because his head can only
> go back so far rather than to the side, and something has to
> give; don't go up on your toes when you kick, otherwise
> you'll fall back from the force of the kick; throw back your
> arm fast for more force when you strike; there will be no
> question that you will break his breastplate.

The statements were made dispassionately and matter-of-factly. The training was mechanical and repetitious. The instructor was not talking to people, but to things who must deal with other things.

In spite of the objectification of the opponent, some of the techniques of defense were designed to be more humane than previous techniques. Mace was designed as an intermediate weapon that could be used to subdue a resisting person, instead of the blackjack, which could easily crack a skull. Come-along holds and the use of pressure points were also employed to allow the patrolman to move someone without knocking him senseless.

Nevertheless, these more humane tactics, like so much of what has been discussed, were valued less for their humaneness than for their practical considerations. Come-along techniques were designed to lessen the possibilities of public outrage.

> One person on one violator is acceptable to the public instead
> of the four-man spread-eagle. People expect the cop to be able to
> do come-alongs. They may look curiously, but nobody will
> object. . . . These methods get the job done. One man can do
> a good job. The Columbia University incident was bad with
> four men picking up one protester and pulling in four different
> directions. It looks bad, and it doesn't get the job done.

The concern was not for the well-being of the violator or the officer. Rather it was over how it might look to an out-group member if he should witness the incident.

Interestingly, perhaps the most blatant example of false personalization occurred in a class in which the recruit was being trained for situations involving pain and suffering—first aid. I quote a few statements by the instructor, but in justice to him, these were not the only reasons he offered for learning his subject. Still, they were certainly the most forceful ones.

> Now there is a constant rise of cases where first aid could
> be used. That's one out of every five calls. This is more than
> a reason for just having knowledge of first aid—one out of five
> cases provides an opportunity to impress for our own purposes.
> You go out there and present a cool, calm, professional image,
> what better place to impress people. When you lose them,
> you don't get blamed. If you don't, you get full credit, whether
> you deserve it or not. Why not get into the limelight when the
> opportunity is made? Nine out of ten letters to the commissioner
> are thanking the police department for assisting in an aided case.
>
> One other reason for taking advantage of this opportunity is,
> the more favorably we impress the public out there, the more
> favorably they will look upon pay and fringe benefits. Whether
> we like it or not, we are dependent upon the people. For every
> person we impress favorably, that's one more person who won't
> fight us. Sometimes on a completely selfish level, it helps to
> relate aided cases with the amount of money in our pockets.
> Look at Metropolitan City. They have one of the highest
> salaries in the country.
>
> . . . the public relations opportunities are absolutely tremendous.
> You make every police officer look good.

STEREOTYPY: COMMUNITY AND RACE RELATIONS

The one agency specifically designed to develop harmony between the public and the police department did very little to counter the attitudes toward the public that the recruit learned from his fellow recruits, his instructors, or his own experiences. In fact, the Community Relations program for the recruit seemed to add to or confirm his predispositions. That is, instead of increasing the recruit's tolerance for ideas and behavior that vary from convention, it seemed to increase his feeling of hostility.

The Community Relations program to which the recruit was exposed lasted for the equivalent of two full days and was divided into three sections. One day was devoted to a lengthy lecture on community relations and some role playing. Almost three weeks later, an afternoon was devoted to race relations by means of a lecture followed by a seminar. About a week after that, the program ended with another lecture on community relations.

My analysis deals with the first two sections, since no data were available to determine recruit reactions to the third. Judging from the response in general to the first two classes, all three were probably given the same status as the many others that the recruit tolerated—merely as something he had to go through as part of his training program. Since none of the lectures went too far beyond the "do's" and "don'ts" of courteous interaction, the beneficial impact of all three was probably minimal. Significantly, the first two classes were not just neutral: their intended effects completely boomeranged. Probably, as far as the recruit was concerned, the first two sections confirmed his suspicions about the irrelevance of the Community Relations Squad, added to his hostility toward a depersonalizing public, and reinforced his prejudices against minority groups.

To begin with, the manner in which the lectures were delivered, their content, and the lecturer's ethnic status cast doubt on the instructor's credibility. The fact that the instructor was black prompted one recruit from Megopolis Department to remark, "You know, one fucking thing; every time they discuss this shit, they have a colored guy up there."

If the purpose of the Community Relations program was to counteract the feeling that the public depersonalized the police, or to encourage the recruit to deal with people as individuals in spite of the abuse the police received in return, it was a failure. The seminars that followed one series of lectures illustrate the point.

First, the recruit was told to express himself freely, yet the instructor put the lid on many discussions by his presence alone and by his taking over discussions when they did occur. His subordinates did likewise in their own way, as is shown in the following example.

R_1: What gets me is that I've heard this stuff for three hours, and
I don't agree with it. Take schools, I came from the city,
and I don't see any differences in education except the one's
in the city are a bunch of arrogant bastards!

S: Remember what I said about tax bases?

R_1: Yeah.

S: I think as policemen we should be aware. We don't have to agree
as long as you are aware. Look, if you go in with this attitude,
watch out.

R_2: You said we could be free in here . . . .

S: Well, I meant if he goes on the job with the feelings
of not agreeing.

Second, the recruit seemed antagonistic toward the instructor and
his five subordinates, who led the seminars. The instructor seemed to
be suggesting that there was no conflict between police officers and
citizens that a little courtesy could not eliminate. For example, one
time he put the brakes on a discussion by interrupting with, "What I
think we are getting here is a we-they attitude . . . there is no we-they."
Such a naive view from the recruit's standpoint seemed to ignore the
real problem of community relations. Indeed, there seemed to be
enough evidence from past lessons or from his own experiences to
indicate the irrelevance of the Community Relations program. By fall-
ing back on his own beliefs, unfortunately, the recruit failed to come
to grips with the "real" problem from the community's perspective.
That is, the problems of police-community relations were barely
touched.

Third, if a recruit accepted the misguiding information taught in
these classes, he would be unprepared for actual field situations.

R_1: You don't have to act that way in Negro neighborhoods out
here. It's only in the city where you gotta watch your throat.

R_2: If I was arrested, none of my neighbors would interfere. They
might gather around, but they wouldn't prevent an arrest.
The Negroes do.

R_3: How do you know about Rurban County? You never lived
in Rurban County, how can you talk about Negroes out here?

I've lived here all my life. I've worked in their neighborhoods. I know how they are.

R₂: I've lived here all my life, too. You don't know what it's like in the Negro neighborhoods out here.

R₃: Right. I'm not prejudiced, but if you go into those neighborhoods with the attitude those guys teach here, you're going to get hurt. You probably know better than me about these things, but in prisons, 80 percent of the prisoners are Negro.

RH: Sure, just like 80 percent of them used to be Irish.

R₃: Sure, that's right, but they worked out of it. The biggest riot in the United States was by the Irish over job discrimination, but they didn't burn down welfare buildings.

A specific statement by the instructor further alienated him from the recruit and further demonstrated that the squad was presenting an unrealistic view. When the instructor introduced the five men from the Community Relations Squad who would lead the seminars, he mentioned that these men were tapped for community relations work on the basis of their interpersonal skills; race had not been a consideration. During a lunch period, the following discussion ensued.

R₁: Those guys. Did you hear him say that race wasn't a consideration in the selection of those men? And three of the five are Negro!

R₂: Did you believe him when he said race was no selective factor?

R₃: But they have to know languages.

R₁: What languages do they know?

R₃: Well, Spanish.

R₁: Yeah, but what about the three Negroes? Do they know Swahili or something?

The biggest complaint by the recruit seemed to revolve around the question of why the public or minority groups do not change *their* attitudes toward the police. The answers he received seemed to skirt the issue. Indeed, the answers demonstrated to him that the Community Relations officers were not really interested in the man on the beat. Instead of convincing out-groups to reevaluate their attitudes, they were asking the recruit to adjust to the police critics.

R: You talk about our attitudes. What about theirs before you even start?

I: Initially you have to be the one to keep your cool. Just be
     supercool, firm, but also respectful and courteous. If you
     retaliate in the same way, you've blown your whole call.
     Because you are the one to lose control of the situation,
     we may have to call another officer.

R: How do you handle the public when it's discourteous to you
     and distorts everything for his benefit.

I: That's the psychological warfare we are up against. I can't
     tell you. It depends on you and the situation. There will be
     many things you will be called: pig, m.f. . . . .

R: Don't the people want to know our gripes, or only their side?

I: We try to show them both sides of the fence. The more
     information channeled in both ways, they'll understand us
     and we'll come to understand them . . . . You've got to take
     it without being personal.

But it is just this point that the recruit is questioning. Does the public
actually want the information "channeled" to it, or does it refuse to
listen? Does the public care about the police point of view? If not, a
one-sided change would be unfair. One squad member warned the
recruit to be careful of phrases he might use which could be inflam-
matory.

     "You people!" "Boy!" "Chico!" "These people!" These are the
     words to avoid. We had one officer at an accident ask quite
     innocently to the crowd, "Will you people please move back?"
     Right away someone in the crowd stepped up, "What do you
     mean, 'you people!' " This is a very sensitive area.

This request seemed unfair to the recruit, for the remark "you people"
was used by everyone, including minority group members and a
squad member who used it automatically when he referred to the
recruit class. Anyone's taking exception to such a phrase during an
accident, he thought, must only be doing so as an excuse to cause
trouble.

One recruit asked if it might help if critics of the police rode around
with patrolmen for a while to get an idea of what police work entails.

I: We tried to get people to ride with us, but they either get tired
     or feel like Uncle Toms and don't stay long enough.

R: Can't they elect their real representatives?

I: It doesn't help. There are too many groups sprouting up, and each one attacks the others and sets itself up as the representative of the community.

Afterward a recruit asked me, "I don't see why we always have to give something to them. Why is it always us who have to give something?"

The apparent feeling by the recruit that he is expected to "give in" to unreasonable requests by police critics, without receiving any understanding in return, contributes to the hostility directed toward out-groups. Members of out-groups want to be treated as individuals without treating police officers as individuals who also have needs and ideas. Consequently, the out-groups, categorized and stereotyped, blend into one formless mass.

By perceiving people stereotypically, the patrolman might endanger himself needlessly, as the following conversation indicates. It also highlights another negative consequence of preparing for the one out of a thousand times "when it counts."

R_1: Why do we always have to change our attitude? Why don't they change their attitude?

I: Look, it doesn't hurt to be courteous. Knock softly, identify yourself, and be courteous unless he shows himself to be belligerent. Would you follow the same way for a Robbery I warrant as for an old lady?

R_1: Yes.

R_2: But you may go on a V & T [a traffic violation] and find a killer.

I: That's the breaks of the game. We don't get beat up on the important things; it's always the little ones. . . . Let's use a little sense in these things. Most police officers get hurt when they are in plainclothes by not identifying themselves and announcing their authority.

By not discriminating between persons of different characteristics, the recruit would be endangering himself. It is not the big arrests in which the officer is hurt, because he is prepared for the unexpected and correctly defines a dangerous situation. He is hurt on arrests for minor offenses by defining danger where none exists.

The recruit seemed to feel in a bind. On the one hand, he is told to treat people alike. On the other hand, he is told to deal with a situation according to its special circumstances. Lacking formal guidelines, he must rely on his own discretion. Quite naturally, he opts for the alternative that seems safest for himself—by imposing his authority immediately and forcefully. However, this response is self-fulfilling: it makes an undangerous situation dangerous. To teach the recruit that there were several alternative responses to a situation, the academy employed the technique of role playing.

EMPATHIC INSENSITIVITY: ROLE PLAYING

During academy training, the recruit was exposed to two classes of role playing. As a teaching technique, it has the potential for encouraging tolerance, empathy, and "personalization," but it, too, seemed to reinforce the depersonalizing tendency as I define it. But first, a description of the mechanics of the role plays is in order.

About 15 recruits were selected by the staff to participate in role-playing situations. As each recruit took part in the role-playing episode on the drill floor, the rest of the class watched the scene over closed-circuit television. The instructors played civilian parts, while the recruits played only police officers. All recruits were given a picture of the scene that a role player would come across, but in addition to what the role player was told, the observers were informed of the background of the episode. For example, one role player was told he would come upon a fight in an all-white neighborhood between three white youth and one black youth who was wielding a car antenna. What the rest of the class knew was that the three whites had provoked the fight. The pattern set by the staff was to have each episode repeated but with another recruit. After the two back-to-back role plays were completed, the staff and invited field sergeants led an evaluation period.

The discussion of role playing as it relates to depersonalization may be broken down into two sections: its technical orientation, and its establishment of a collection of vicarious experiences.

TECHNICAL ROLE PLAYING. Role playing is commonly divided into two types. In one, the psychodrama, the subject is asked to act out a role in which he plays himself. In the second type, the sociodrama, the subject plays the part of someone else. In each case, the subject reveals something about his attitudes toward himself and toward others.

I prefer a different breakdown into what I call "emphatic role playing" and "technical role playing." Both orientations crosscut the psychodrama and sociodrama. If role playing is empathic, it does not matter if the subject plays himself or another. The purposes of empathic role playing include (1) the learning of new perspectives that can open up new paths of communication between people, (2) the development of the subject's capacity for taking the role of the other (empathy), (3) the development of tolerance for unconventional attitudes and behavior, (4) the learning of a repertoire of responses to facilitate empathy, and (5) the gaining of insight into the subject's own attitudes and beliefs. All of the above would seem to counteract depersonalizing tendencies.

In contrast to empathic role playing is technical role playing. Less oriented toward developing empathy and self-understanding, it is predominantly instrumental: a subject learns techniques in order to improve his job performance. In the case of RCPD role playing, most of the role plays were designed to teach the recruit how best to handle situations that he might encounter in his role as patrolman. Role plays included handling drunks and loitering youths, giving speeding tickets with a minimum of danger to oneself and to the occupants of the speeding car, following proper procedures when finding a burglary in progress, and handling family disputes.

Although a few role plays were designed to challenge some stereotypes held by the recruit, the emphasis still seemed to be on the technical—the harmful consequences of his false perceptions on himself. In any case, the empathic orientation was less dominant than the technical orientation. In every instance, the recruit seemed to be sympathetic toward the white role player even when the black role player was clearly in the right. Although the recruit seemed to rebel against instruction in Community Relations, he seemed to recognize the need for role plays in police training; but even his comments were technically oriented. His suggestions included the following: (1) role plays should include struggling in order to test the recruit's ability for self-defense, (2) role playing should be applied to every subject such as robbery and assault, and (3) role plays should include situations in which a recruit must apply his knowledge of the law. In no case did I hear a recruit express a desire to learn more about himself or others through role playing.

REPERTOIRE OF RESPONSES. If there was any value to the role playing, it at least added to the recruit's collection of experiences. Each role play exposed the recruit to a vicariously experienced facet of police work. For instance, after a role play on family disputes, the recruit learned that he should always separate the couple into different rooms of the house and that he could not throw a man out of his own house without the wife's signing a complaint.

One particular role play left a powerful impression on the class and prompted one recruit to exclaim, "Screw traffic—this is your life!" The role play consisted of three recruits who were called to a burglary in progress. Since it was nighttime, the best we could make out were some shadows on the television screen. One recruit was searching a suspect while the second recruit was standing over both of them with his gun drawn. Suddenly three shots rang out (wax bullets were used). We jumped from surprise, and sounds of "oh, oh" went around the room. Some minutes later, the role players returned to the classroom, and we began the analysis.

The search was bad. There was another gun, and I had a knife on my arm. Don't be close enough to touch a suspect's back with your gun. If you tell him not to move, and he moves, that's it.
If a burglar is running away other than Burglary I, and he hasn't a dangerous weapon, doesn't threaten you with harm, or an innocent person is not endangered, you cannot kill him.

What had happened was that one of the suspects was "killed" trying to escape. The suspect who was being searched made a movement, and the recruit who was watching the search shot both the suspect and his own partner in the excitement. If this episode had been real, an officer would have been killed by his own partner. And this occurred just two weeks before graduation!

Collecting a repertoire of vicarious experiences could be beneficial to the recruit in another sense. Earlier it was pointed out that the recruit tended to choose, when in a potentially dangerous situation, a line of action that frequently endangered him even more. (Remember, I am speaking of the relatively insecure recruit, not the patrolman who has acquired more "know how.") The instructors tried desperately to show the recruit that he actually had several alternatives from which to choose—all of which would have been less dangerous.

For example, the recruit seemed to feel that his gun was his first line of defense, not his last. In the following excerpt, the recruit's tendency to neglect several lines of action that were open to him seemed to be wrapped up in his concept of himself as a man of action. The role-play episode referred to was about a recruit who had to handle a belligerent speeding driver and his passenger. An instructor warned the class that an officer could not legally use his gun in this instance because no felony had been committed.

R_1: What's wrong with 'jacking him?

I: Well, the mace was designed to see that the 'jack wouldn't
       be needed. Just be prepared to take him to a hospital to put
       some stitches in his head if you use a 'jack.

R₂: What are you supposed to do if he [the driver] takes off
       [while you're writing the ticket]?

I: So he takes off. You have his name, rank, and license number.
       And chase him again. Don't get clobbered. If he gets out
       of the car to clobber you, just go back to your own car
       and roll up the window, and call for help.

R₃: I have a question for the road sergeants. In a real situation,
       do you call for help, or will the whole squad be talking about it?

I: Whenever it reduces to physical force, you call for assistance . . . .
       You have a whole army at the end of the "mike," and they're
       all on your side. The important thing is to take care of yourself
       on [vehicle and traffic violations].

The same kind of question came up in earlier role play.

R: Why not pull the gun out and say, shut the fuck up? Why take it
       [badgering]?

I: Brother, that's bad business . . . What are you going to do,
       have someone say "screw you" and pull out your gun?
       Never use a gun for psychological effect today. If you draw it,
       use it. The gun is always a last resort. Don't use it as the
       first choice.

In both of the above examples the recruit seemed to think that his
personal authority was being challenged if someone tried to "get
away" with an offense. To retreat from a belligerent driver, or from
the mocking by two drunks, or from a person who used the officer's
own mace on him, would be too damaging to the recruit's self-image
as a man of action to let it pass without proving who was in authority.
Even if he exposed himself to greater danger, the recruit seemed to
feel safer using his gun to bring the culprit to justice. Perhaps, he
would be safer or, perhaps, he would cause a manageable situation
to result in injury or death to one of the parties. The role plays provided the recruit with some awareness that alternatives were open
to him, but because of the limited use of role playing throughout the
training session, the message was lost on, at least, a few recruits. An
example is this comment regarding a role play about a belligerent
driver:

> When you [R$_2$] had him up against the car, that would have
> been the end of it. If he wasn't a cop, he'd be on the floor. That's
> why I say it can't be done on television.

Apparently, he did not realize that the point of the lesson was that
no physical force was necessary in the first place. As soon as the
driver got out of the car to fight, the recruit could have merely gone
to the protection of his own car.

In conclusion, several classes had the potential to counteract recruit
depersonalization of out-groups. In spite of wholesome attempts by
some instructors to increase the recruit's capacity to take the role
of the other (empathize), their efforts were largely overwhelmed by
the recruit's acceptance of the defensive ethos and of the narrow
definition of the professional image. Role playing did, at least, provide
the recruit with experience in handling problematic situations in more
than one way.

Although the academy staff welcomed speakers who would present
opposing viewpoints, it appeared that any controversial speaker was
reserved for in-service trainees. Except during the morning made available to me, there were no discussions at all that presented ideas contrary to convention as legitimate, honest, or idealistic. Often attitudes
and behavior that seemed to deviate from the recruit's standard of
convention were disparaged. During one lecture an officer told a
story about a physicist who always threatened suicide.

> Well, he finally killed himself. Even though we deal with it all
> the time, we try to be respectful. "Would you like us to call a
> priest?" We don't believe in God!" "Okay, what do you want
> us to do with this piece of shit?" (Laughter)

Apparently such a remark was deemed legitimate, since the widow
had not behaved respectfully toward religion. Thus it is no wonder
that the recruit will find it hard to communicate with out-group members once he leaves the police academy. It seemed that even the most
enlightened classes were functionally related to the maintenance of
depersonalization.

DEPERSONALIZATION AND SOLIDARITY

Depersonalization is a two-way process. It goes beyond intrapsycho-
logical issues, since it finds expression in interpersonal relationships
and in the social structure. In the case of the police recruit, he feels
depersonalized by out-groups, the social structure, and the depart-

ment; and he depersonalizes, too. He is stereotyped, and he stereotypes in return. Upholding the substantive laws of society, he is castigated if he deviates from procedural law. In a power position as actor,
he feels acted upon. Craving to be accepted, he finds himself isolated.
Indeed, citizen and policeman seem to have a mutual pact to segregate
themselves from each other through symbolic and physical barriers.
Cut off from "normal" human interaction, uncomfortable when attending civilian parties if his occupation is known, forced to perform his
duties with little outside help or compliance, the officer, coming from
one narrow cultural ledge, withdraws to another narrow cultural
ledge of, by, and for fellow policemen. The police officer is left to his
own devices to manage as best he can, since to look on the police
officer as a person means becoming involved in his work. If the citizen
does not become involved in police work, he does not have to accept
the responsibility for resolving the officer's dilemmas.

The recruit learns that his social identity is equated with his occupational identity; even when he is in civilian clothes, he is a cop. Finding
himself isolated from the community, he turns toward his in-group for
emotional support, psychological defense, and his cues for action or
inaction. As a consequence of a training program that is based on the
experiences of others, the recruit also learns that the only ones he has
to love are his colleagues. Only among his fellow officers is the recruit
personalized and personalizing.

During my closing days at the academy when I realized I would
have to make the transition from recruit back to student, I obtained
further insights into personalization among the recruits. Two days
before graduation, the recruits took their qualifying tests at the pistol
range. Without scoring 200 out of a possible 300 points, they could
not graduate. A staff member visited us at the range for a short while,
but during that time he said he had to turn in my shield and "the time
has come for you to be defrocked." I knew I would have to turn in
my shield sometime, but his request caught me by surprise because I
thought I would be able to keep it for another day. Also, I had grown
rather attached to the shield, secretly hoping I could keep it as a
memento of my experiences. But the police would rather lose a gun
than lose a shield. As I unpinned the shield, I tried to joke, "I want
you to know I'm taking this personally."

When word of my shield spread among the recruits, they acted
surprised, "They took your badge?" Some of them sympathized with
me as I moped around, "They took your shield?" I forced a smile,
"Yeah, I've been defrocked." "Aw, you'll always be one of the boys,
you know that." Two men from Megopolis City tried to cheer me up

with plans for my wearing their old blue uniforms during our last inspection the next day.

The next day I walked into the academy with part of a uniform from Megopolis City. We figured that we would have one last inspection in our gray uniforms, but there never was one. So the two men who put together my uniform literally pushed me into the staff's office to get their response. It was as if the taking of my shield symbolized the beginning of the end of the class identity. The prank could be perceived as a plea, "See, he has a blue uniform, too, just like the rest of us will wear tomorrow." At lunch time I gloomily turned in my equipment except for my two uniforms which I was allowed to keep. As I passed some recruits, they called out, "Getting cashiered, Harris?"

Later in the afternoon, we went to Community College for a rehearsal of our graduation ceremony. As the recruits went through the mock presentations of their certificates while I sat alone, the full significance that I was no longer a part of the group and never could be again hit me. The only consolation I could think of was that in 24 hours, even if I were a recruit, the class would be dispersed forever anyway.

On the day of graduation, the sergeant came up to me when I arrived and said the inspector wanted to see me. On the way to the auditorium he said, "You have done something I never expected you to be able to do; I had my biases, too, but they really accepted you." I replied, "I'm going to miss them, too." Inside, the inspector told me there was a chair for me on the stage for the ceremony. He introduced me to a few officials, and then I asked to be excused in order to be with the recruits.

Outside, the recruits, soon to be rookies, were milling around in their blue uniforms. I joked, "Hey, even Carter looks like a cop." They joked back, "Hey, you really look relaxed in your suit," and "Why aren't you in blues, Harris?" "I'm a detective." Each of us was adjusting himself to his new role toward each other.

The men fell in for their last roll call as a class. I stood up front leaning on one of the patrol cars in the roadway. Some of the men called out, "Hey, get in line, Harris," but I politely declined with a wave of my hand. However, during roll call, my squad leader reported to our platoon sergeant, "One man missing, sir!" I gave in, and took my regular position within ranks. The platoon sergeant reported to the staff, "One man missing, but accounted for, sir!" I stayed in formation a couple of minutes, but feeling awkward in my civilian clothes, I left ranks for good.

After the graduation ceremony, while preparing to leave, I noticed the rookies gathering in the first three rows in front of the stage. The sergeant called me over, "Come on down, you're part of this, too." The class president was saying something on the stage, but I was not listening. I was still confused because I understood that immediately following graduation the rookies were to meet with their precinct commanders. Then I heard my name called. I stood up uncertainly, but the men started clapping and told me to go up on the stage. As I headed toward the president I saw a wooden plaque in his hand. Before I accepted it, I saluted him in the same manner in which the recruits had saluted the commissioner when they received their diplomas. My behavior took the president off balance, but he returned the salute while the class laughed. The plaque had a brass inscription and below it was my S-191 shield. In spite of my being a little choked up, the men demanded I make a speech, so I gave a short but emotional one.

This experience was very meaningful to me as a person and as a researcher. First, it indicated that I really had been accepted by the recruits, something I had yearned for but never felt. The recruits had themselves petitioned the commissioner to release the shield to me that I had worn throughout the academy. Second, it represented that there was something special about our class that created a unifying bond for all of us: it was not just another step in our careers. Third, it helped bridge the transition back to my school life and made it easier and smoother. The plaque took on more meaning to me at the graduation party that night when the lieutenant told me that it was unprecedented to retire a shield for a civilian and rare for an actual policeman.

As for the graduation party itself, its significance lies in its heightened expression of solidarity, which first seemed to emerge when my badge was taken away from me. Even the recruit who had most vociferously disrupted the plans for the party, along with another recruit who had also refused to participate, felt the need to visit it for a short while. Apparently symbolic of the class identity, I became the center of attention that night. Recruits introduced me to their wives, they came up to me individually and said they were happy to have known me, and—the biggest compliment for me—the most antistudent recruit of them all admitted that since meeting me his attitudes about students and long-hairs had changed and that, perhaps, some of their demands had merit. The great sense of solidarity expressed at the graduation party was, to some extent, the other side of the negativism, violence, and depersonalization that the recruits had to look forward to every day of their working lives. The recruits who had been skeptical about their recruit role and classroom training, retrospectively embraced the program—and each other.

Involvement is necessary to understand the psychological
realities of a culture, that is, its meanings
for the indigenous members. Detachment is necessary
to construct the abstract reality: a network of social
relations including the rules and how they function—
not necessarily real to the people studied.
Hortense Powdermaker, Stranger and Friend

Summary and Conclusions.

CHAPTER SIX

SUMMARY

The policeman in our society is in a precarious position. Operating in what he believes to be a hostile environment, he is often faced with situations in which he must rely on his own discretion. While he is expected to enforce laws impartially, he finds that there are many ambiguous and contradictory laws without clear guidelines for his behavior. If there are guidelines, they usually state what the officer cannot do, not what he can do.

Not only must the officer engage in law enforcement activities, such as responding to burglaries and homicides, he is also expected to engage in peace maintenance, such as handling family disputes and disorderly conduct. Indeed, a growing literature indicates that only 10 to 15 percent of police time is spent in law enforcement activities.[1] In maintaining peace and order, the policeman must use discretion to determine the best way to prevent a problem of order from possibly developing into a problem that requires arrest. Furthermore, the disputants themselves may want the officer to resolve a predicament, not by making an arrest but by "handling the situation." Consequently, when he either enforces the law or maintains the peace, the policeman is forced—or has the opportunity—to rely on his judgment in choosing among several possible options. In these situations, where

---

[1] Elaine Cumming, I. M. Cumming, and L. Edell, "The Policeman as Philosopher, Guide and Friend," *Social Problems* (Winter 1965), pp. 276–286; James Q. Wilson, *Varieties of Police Behavior* (Cambridge, Mass.: Harvard University, 1968); and Egon Bittner, "The Police on Skid-Row: A Study of Peace-Keeping," *American Sociological Review*, 32 (October 1967), pp. 699–715.

there is no one "right" choice (if any), the option taken may reflect his personal preferences. The officer then becomes vulnerable to criticisms from those of other persuasions, no matter what he decides to do.

One of the main purposes of the police academy seemed to be to develop uniform behavior within the department in order to lessen the member's need to depend on his own judgment. In a few instances the training tried to broaden the officer's range of options, but the general rule was to narrow it. Some of the techniques that were used to encourage uniform behavior were external discipline, written rules and procedures, a reporting system, and an Inspection Squad. Standardized behavior seemed to have two consequences for the department: it lessened the number of decisions that an officer had to make, and it protected the department from public criticism.

During his 12-week training period, the recruit was exposed to a range of content areas: law, self-defense, first aid, functions of departmental divisions, formal rules and procedures, community relations, and patrol procedures. However, three major themes were apparent in all these content areas. The intertwined themes—defensiveness, professionalization, and depersonalization—seemed to operate on the levels of police-community interaction, the police organization, and the individual policeman. Not only did the themes reflect problems of police work but also they represented resolutions to these problems. In the case of depersonalization, for example, the problem from the point of view of the officer was interacting with a depersonalizing public; he adapted by depersonalizing the public in return. Indeed, the recruits used the values implied by the themes for evaluating and judging both himself and others. The only apparent difference between instructor and recruit regarding these three themes was that the instructor had more experience and was better able to articulate his feelings and beliefs. Concerns of the recruits that seemed linked to the themes and that were revealed in their informal conversations included maintaining the man-of-action image, improving their occupational and financial status, and seeing to it that "crime does not pay."

The recruit learned that he would be vulnerable to occupational dangers that he apparently had not foreseen. He probably accepted the inherent dangers of patrol work and law enforcement, but he seemed to expect more support and protection by his department. The mechanisms that the department established to protect the patrolman seemed to be perceived as presenting additional threats to his personal and occupational safety, such as Inspection and Community Relations. In addition to his department, the recruit learned to be wary of specific groups on apparently sound police experience. It was not so much that members of these groups and other citizens would go out of their way to endanger the policeman as it was their expected willingness to report his mistakes or indiscretions whenever possible. Consequently, the recruit learned that in the last analysis he could only depend on his fellow patrolmen. As the sense of in-group solidarity increased, a tendency toward uninvolvement in citizen foibles and character weaknesses also increased. To maintain in-group loyalty, legal deviations and a code of secrecy seemed to be informally sanctioned.

While the courts and citizen watchdogs were believed to restrict the policeman's territory of action, the departmental hierarchy and the rank-and-file members tried to extend their sphere of autonomy. The prime means to convince the public that RCPD should have more autonomy and that its members were worthy of higher salaries was through professionalism. By professionalizing police work, the department hoped to raise the quality of police officers and the status of police work. The police academy training program seemed to be offered as proof that only a special person could join law enforcement—not just anybody could be a police officer. However, the recruit and his instructors seemed to take only the "shell" of professionalism, not its core. Outward conformity seemed more important than attitudinal conformity. The problem was exacerbated by the lack of a clear definition of professionalism.

If the police were trying to convince the public that they were professional, they were probably quite correct to focus on superficial criteria such as demeanor and physical appearance that were closely aligned with the professional image. The public is generally ignorant of what is involved in most occupations; therefore, external appearances provide the only bases by which they can evaluate an occupation. Unfortunately for the police, the historical image of the police officer that seems to be held by the public is unfavorable to them. Through professionalization, the police are trying to replace this image with a more favorable one. However, the three components of the professional image do not seem to be operating when the police must deal with political protesters, be they violent or nonviolent. Perhaps if they extend courtesy and expand their definitions of morality within group confrontations, instead of merely to one-to-one situations, the desired image will become more acceptable to the public.

Nevertheless, even if the public defined police officers as professionals, some of the significant problems of police work would probably not be dissipated, contrary to what many officers expect. There is evidence which suggests that members of "professional" police departments display little difference in behavior from those of "non-professional" departments.[2] As Wilson observes, "the ethos of professionalism assumes that the impersonal rules of law enforcement are correct and appropriate regardless of what a hostile or indifferent citizenry may think," thereby lessening the value that the police place on public opinion. A few scholars also observe a general tendency of client rejection of policy decisions made by professionals: patients criticize doctors, students reject teachers, and residents organize against urbanologists.[3] Clients recognize their need for professional help with their problems, but they object to professionals' determining policy. The clients themselves want the right to determine their own needs; professionals, they claim, should use their skills to provide the means to these goals. Notably, this seems to be the present predicament of police agencies vis-à-vis the community. Although citizen respect and police salaries may increase, the police should not expect a decrease in citizen complaints regarding their decisions—there may even be an increase.

As part of the department's attempt to convince the recruit that he was a professional within a profession, he was told that he was unique and that he was far better than members of elite professions. The feeling of solidarity through shared uniqueness, however, also cut off the recruit from interacting with out-group members on an equal or respectful basis. The recruit's separation from the citizenry was increased as he became ingrained with suspicion, distrust, and envy. As a result of these feelings, the recruit tended to depersonalize the citizenry. In turn, his apparent emotional and psychological isolation from the public made it easier for the public to stereotype him.

Because the instructors concentrated on outward signs of professionalism, the recruit sensed that they really did not believe in professionalism except as a means of obtaining public support, monies, and respect. If the training period were doubled or even tripled, its

---

[2] James Q. Wilson, "Police Morale, Reform, and Citizen Respect: The Chicago Case," The Police, edited by David J. Bordua (New York: John Wiley, 1967), pp. 137–162, and "Dilemmas of Police Administration," Public Administration Review, 28 (September–October 1968), pp. 407–417; and Michael Banton, The Policeman in the Community (New York: Basic Books, 1965), pp. 159–161.

[3] Marie R. Haug and Marvin B. Sussmann, "Professional Autonomy and the Revolt of the Client," Social Problems, 17 (Fall 1969), pp. 153–161; and Elliott A. Krause, "Functions of a Bureaucratic Ideology: 'Citizen Participation'," Social Problems, 16 (Fall 1968), pp. 129–143.

effects on the recruit would probably remain the same. The kind of law enforcer who emerged from the police academy was the same kind as his counterpart of just a few years ago except that the modern officer may be better trained and more sensitive to his appearance and demeanor. Shrouding the same person in different clothes fools no one. The department might be able to alter the physical image of the police stereotype, but it unintentionally (intentionally?) reinforces the old ideology—the beliefs that unconventional attitudes and behavior are not to be tolerated and that due process of law should be subordinate to order.

For instance, lectures seemed to be one-sided; they did not offer informed presentations of unconventional ideologies. According to class presentations, the real harm of Chicago's police riot of 1968 was that "it didn't look good" although the demonstrators "got what they deserved." Lectures on marijuana were propagandistic. Supreme Court decisions were presented as opposed to the ideals of justice—they must be obeyed because it is a requirement, not because it is legally or democratically correct. Interestingly, the lectures on community relations, which were geared toward challenging the basic assumptions of the recruit, seemed to fail dismally and only succeeded in confirming his biases and preexisting attitudes. If the police department wants to change the image of police work and police officers, it must do more than have its men change their physical appearances. There must also be a change in attitude that leads to more meaningful changes in behavior.

CONCLUSIONS

SOLIDARITY

Of several unanticipated and unrecognized consequences of police training, one of the most significant was the cultivation of solidarity. By solidarity, I mean consensus, integration, friendship, personal intimacy, emotional depth, moral commitment, and continuity in time.[4] It is a subjective feeling of belongingness and implication in each other's lives. Indeed, solidarity seemed to be instilled in the recruits by

---

[4] Émile Durkheim, *The Division of Labor in Society*, trans., George Simpson (Glencoe, Ill.: Free Press, 1947); and Robert A. Nisbet, *The Sociological Tradition* (New York: Basic Books, 1966), pp. 47–48.

means of defensiveness, professionalization, and depersonalization.

The defensive ethos reflects in-group/out-group tensions and adaptations. The solidarity which emanates from this theme provides the patrolman with moral support in performing his duties. Without the confidence of knowing that someone is always ready to help in dangerous or sticky situations, the officer might hesitate in acting at all. Often he must put, or thinks he must put, his life on the line. The occupational necessity of having workers who have a strong sense of solidarity creates the need for in-group/out-group distinctions. The sentiment of an in-group is that of peace and cooperation within itself, but of suspicion, hostility, and distrust of those outside the group.[5] Consequently, modes of adaptation on individual and group levels are established to help the patrolman interact with out-group members without psychological or emotional wear-and-tear.

The heavy emphasis on professionalization may be interpreted as a mechanism for creating a sense of belonging, of we-ness. The members of an in-group have a common interest against other groups. In-group solidarity connotes loyalty against criticism—even if it is from another officer. Sometimes, however, an in-group member may do something to incur the wrath of the other members. During one of the physical training periods, for example, the recruits began throwing a football back and forth while they were running laps around the drill floor. One recruit picked up the dropped ball and placed it back on the table from which it was taken. When this move proved unsuccessful, he picked up the ball again and this time put it in the staff's office. Said one recruit, referring to the time when the class would be assigned to precincts, "The word is out on him; at least they'll find out about him, that bastard." Solidarity seemed so important that colleagues had to be warned about someone who threatened that solidarity, since he probably could not be depended on in connection with more important issues. No one must challenge the solidarity of the group, not even another police officer.

If in-group solidarity is reflected in the theme of professionalization, the way in which the police tend to respond to out-groups is reflected in the theme of depersonalization. Depersonalization seems to crystallize the out-group by defining anybody outside of the in-group as objects. Perhaps certain elements of depersonalization are consequences of the need for police efficiency, time pressures, and impartial

---

[5] William Graham Sumner, *Folkways* (New York: American Library, 1940), p. 27.

law enforcement. Nevertheless, an officer can be impartial and *still* be either depersonalizing or personalizing. In this respect, it is the *quality* of impersonal interaction that is relevant. While impartial and impersonal law enforcement is defined by most reform-minded police officials as professional, police training seems to dispose patrolmen to react intolerantly and depersonally toward out-group members.

The configuration of solidarity is found in other training programs as well. Sanford Dornbusch reports in his participatory study of the Coast Guard Academy that informal rules take precedence over written rules and regulations in order to preserve feelings of group solidarity. He cites an instance in which a cadet was not expelled for breaking an important regulation because his classmates petitioned for him to stay.[6] The hazing process of training also contributes to solidarity. The technique is used by groups, such as the military, as well as social fraternities. In each case, hazing is believed to separate the "men from the boys." In each case, solidarity connotes certain premises are to remain unquestioned. The recruit learns that rank has its privilege, and more subtly, the fraternity "pledge" learns not to be too independent. The "system" must remain unchallenged at all costs.

If the development of solidarity is a latent function of training programs, then the complaints of trainees that much of their training is irrelevant to their needs takes on added proportions. For example, I am told by an insider that until they become interns, medical students have not learned to give shots to patients. College students are forced to take courses for which, at the time, they believe they will never have any use. Police recruits seemed to believe that they had to wait until the completion of their academy training before their "real" training would begin.

Perhaps the recruit hit a spark of truth (but only a spark, for those who may think that this is evidence for abolishing police training) when he claimed academy training was "just a waste of time." He argued that there was little relationship between the in vitro classroom situation and the in vivo activities of police work. This study has shown that there is, at least, one great and direct relationship: the lessons cultivate group solidarity.

---

[6] Sanford Dornbusch, "The Military Academy as an Assimilating Institution," *Social Forces*, 33 (May 1955), pp. 316–321.

ROLE DISTANCE

Another question that this study may help to answer is: Does police training encourage the recruit to accept the police image that the department claims it wants?

Erving Goffman outlines a significant concept called role distance which, unfortunately, has not received as much attention as it could. Role distance refers to "actions which effectively convey some disdainful detachment of the performer from the role he is performing." It occurs when an individual consciously plays a role tongue-in-cheek; he does what is expected of him, but simultaneously he maintains an inner distance with respect to his role. The role player may show distance from his role because he wants to protect himself from the psychological dangers of complete embracement. For instance, if he does not fully commit himself to a standard of achievement, he does not have to be judged entirely by an incompetent act. The person uses any means available to introduce a "margin of freedom of maneuverability" in order to maintain a distinction between his "real" self and the role-defined self. In effect, he demonstrates that he refuses to be defined by what is officially in progress. The performer does not deny the role: he is really denying the self that is totally defined by the role. If, on the other hand, the performer "embraces" the role instead of taking distance from it, he perceives his identity only in terms of a role category, and believes others to see him similarly.[7]

The police academy aims at developing competence among its new members, and it tries to do this through formal courses. The problem, however, is that much of police work cannot be formally taught. Recognizing this, the recruit seemed to reject not the image of patrolman, but the image of student-recruit. One way in which the recruit unconsciously expressed disdain for the academy image was by mocking it, as illustrated in the ethic of masculinity discussion. Through what would be thought of as a breakdown in discipline (or horseplay) on an overt level, the typical recruit seemed to be rebelling against the student spit-and-polish image. However, before the recruit finally left the academy, a staff member offered some advice. Implicit in his suggestions was the awareness that the recruit role was a temporary rite de passage.

> ... don't come on too strong. Don't put in suggestions in the
> beginning, don't come in like gang-busters. You may have good

---

[7] Erving Goffman, "Role Distance," *Encounters* (Indianapolis: Bobbs-Merrill, 1961), pp. 84–152.

intentions, but it won't be received like that. Look the part. You are going to be judged. They won't think you're a baby; they expect it from you. "Sir" them to death. They expect it in the beginning.

Perhaps any training program has an element of role distance for its trainees simply because the trainee role is a transitory stage. For example, a study of medical school training reports that students are not permitted to take courses that they believe necessary for their career until their advanced training stages.[8] Like recruits, medical students value experience and responsibility; only when they may make unsupervised decisions do they feel free to embrace the professional image of doctor. However, making decisions without experience may be frightening when other people's lives are involved. The medical student can resolve his dilemma by specializing in one area of medicine. That way he only needs to command a portion of medical knowledge. The police recruit does not have this alternative. He is, in essence, a general practitioner; he is responsible for a wide range of activities in which the public expects him to be expert. Nevertheless, the only way to obtain this experience is by beginning field work as soon as possible. In rejecting the student-recruit role, the recruit embraces the patrolman role, which is the ultimate purpose anyway.

The problem in RCPD is that the relationship between transitory recruit role and committed patrolman role is not so clear cut. The police department declares that it wants to mold in-coming members into a new breed of police officer. If this statement is accurate, then the recruit role could be expected to help the in-coming member embrace this new police image. But it is not at all clear that the department knows what the new image is or even if it really wants the new image. Surely the police academy training reflects this ambivalence. The effect on the recruit in taking distance from the "new" role and image implied in the official academy training is that he embraces the "old" police role and image, which seemed to be implied in the undercurrents of academy training.

Some of the recruit's instructors fed his belief that the role he was supposed to play during his 12 weeks of training was not appropriate to the patrolman image. Various instructors would interrupt their lectures to make snide comments about the content of their lectures or to mention that the recruit would learn how to con people or evade due

---

[8] Howard S. Becker et al., *Boys in White* (Chicago: University of Chicago, 1961), pp. 382–383.

process of law once he left the academy. One instructor happened to encourage the recruit to detach himself from the impact of his lecture about the dangers of carrying a revolver. He ended his quite serious lecture with a few sexual jokes. What he really seemed to be saying —other than the obvious point of relaxing the recruits after an anxiety provoking lecture—was to inform them that things were not as bad as they might think.

A similar process occurs during daily news reports. A television broadcast can graphically show a starving American in the ghetto, an American atrocity in Vietnam, killings of students at Jackson State College and Kent State College, or politicians in high office who actively stimulate social injustices. But there is always the commercial that follows. It tells the listener, "Look, things aren't that bad. Our commercial is the real world; our product proves it. We advertised it yesterday, and we'll advertise it tomorrow. The world will survive an increase in the nuclear arms race and the American invasion of Cambodia. Just sit back and use our dangerous automobiles, our poisonous foods, or our tampons."

In conclusion, the police academy seems to institutionalize role distance by reinforcing and sanctioning the recruit's belief that his training and image in the academy are irrelevant to police work. Before assignment to the academy, each staff member demonstrated in his field work his ability to compatibly integrate his notion of professionalism with the demands of police work. But partially because the staff members were not aware of the underlying processes of training (defensiveness, professionalization, depersonalization, solidarity, a cop-and-robber interactional framework, and the ethics of masculinity and cutting corners), they were actually defeating their intentions by institutionalizing role distance among the recruits.

I began this study by challenging the claim that academy training is either irrelevant to the on-the-job needs of the patrolman or has little lasting effect on the recruit once he leaves the academy. Although my data suggest that my hunch was correct, I still cannot offer a definitive answer. Once I met a former member of the recruit class who was on patrol. He recognized me, but I could not place him, although his face seemed very familiar. I just had not met that many patrolmen during my study of the academy. Obviously, I was trying to remember his face in the wrong context—in his blue uniform. He finally had to tell me his name. The uniform in my mind turned from officer blue to recruit gray and, of course, I recognized him. The contrast between his blue and gray uniforms was symbolic, for me, of the differences between what a policeman does on the job and what he was taught in the academy. And maybe that is the way it really is . . . .

Custom reconciles us to everything.
Edmund Burke, On the Sublime and Beautiful

Policy Implications.

CHAPTER SEVEN

The purpose of my study has been to impartially describe and analyze some of the salient processes and structures of police academy training. Given the present crisis of police-community-protester group interaction, it is important to complete this study with specific recommendations for policy change. Since my recommendations focus only on police training, they could be handicapped without the broader contextual changes suggested by other researchers that I now briefly describe.

Jerome Skolnick, James Wilson, and Peter Manning, among others, maintain that there can be no resolution of police problems, without the sacrifice of democratic principles, unless other cultural and structural changes occur.[1] They argue that the police are subject to a confused and contradictory mandate. On the one hand, they are to enforce substantive law while constrained both by procedural law and departmental rules and regulations. On the other hand, they must maintain order by handling situations according to their own discretion with little or no formal guidelines. Because the public seems to evaluate police performance and efficiency along law enforcement lines, the police respond by subordinating due process of law in order to preserve their conception of order.

Skolnick, Wilson, and Manning offer their combined proposals as

---

[1] Jerome H. Skolnick, *Justice Without Trial* (New York: John Wiley, 1966); James Q. Wilson, *Varieties of Police Behavior* (Cambridge, Mass.: Harvard University, 1968); and Peter K. Manning, "Police Trouble: Mandate, Strategies and Appearances," edited by Jack D. Douglas, *Crime and Justice in American Society* (Indianapolis: Bobbs-Merrill, 1971), pp. 149–193.

mandatory to any amelioration of police problems. First, the police need a clearly stated and unambiguous mandate. Second, moralistic and unenforceable laws such as those for crimes without victims (prostitution, drug addiction, drunkenness, and gambling) should be stricken from the criminal code. Third, some way by which police departments will be made accountable to the communities they serve must be institutionalized. Finally, police departments should reorganize according to the functional requirements of order maintenance, since up to 80 percent of requests for police aid call for order maintenance rather than law enforcement. Presently, departments are divided along law enforcement lines: burglary, vice, homicide, narcotics, and so forth. Yet it is the uniformed patrolman who is responsible for everything else, which is essentially keeping the peace. Wilson, therefore, suggests one felony squad to handle law-enforcing activities and, for maintaining order, functionally differentiated squads for domestic trouble, drunkenness, and juveniles.

Although I agree with the need for implementing these recommendations, I do not see public officials, citizens, or policemen willing to carry them out. Consequently, my own recommendations may be enhanced by their common weakness, namely, ignoring the broader changes. By focusing only on police training, major changes may be made without upsetting the overall police organization. Perhaps, too, as training techniques change, the broader changes will not be far behind.

Partly because this chapter differs from the previous ones in that it reflects a clear value judgment on my part, I offer my recommendations with some trepidation. Often, when suggestions are made for policy changes within any institution, some of the most necessary changes are ignored or the study is used to initiate changes contradictory to its intentions. One of my fears, in this case, is that some police officials will use my findings to reduce the training program by simply eliminating extraneous courses instead of replacing them with panels, debates, group therapy sessions, and the like. My study had not even been written up when I learned that soon after I had left the academy, the training period of RCPD was streamlined to the bare technicalities—no discussions, no community relations panels, no "unessential" field trips. This is exactly what should not happen, as presently I shall try to make clear.

Perhaps one of the greatest problems of police work lies in gaining broad confidence and support from the public at large, but particularly from critical minority groups, students, and politicians. Skolnick sees part of this problem as resulting from a paramilitary police organization whose members are not really attuned to operating according to democratic and constitutional principles.[2] Indeed, this study suggests that the police perpetuate their own problems. This, I believe, has been clearly demonstrated in police training within one relatively liberal and enlightened department. The police training I experienced reconfirms the need to eliminate technically oriented subjects and to replace them with lessons that emphasize principles of law, democracy, and interpersonal relationships. My impression of police training is that it does not teach recruits an appreciation for democratically based institutions or a tolerance for unconventional behavior and attitudes. The consequence of these limitations seems to be the perpetuation of the stereotypes that the police claim they want to counteract. Divisions are drawn between "we" and "they," and both "we" and "they" are defined in categorical terms.

Both instructor and recruit should examine their self-images as police officers. It is important that they think more carefully about what the label of policeman means, could mean, and should mean. Based on this study, there seem to be several main ways in which police instructor and recruit escape from this self-analysis.

First, the recruit and his instructor are "up-tight" about the tactics of law, rules, and procedures. Rather than think about the general strategies and purposes of their work, the recruit and instructor preoccupy themselves with the means toward their goals instead of the goals themselves. Perhaps it is easier for them to think concretely about the "when," "where," and "how" to act than the more abstract question of "why" they act or should act as they do. Nevertheless, it is the "why" that should be examined.

Second, recruit and instructor seem to wave the flag of professionalism. However, professionalism may be used to mask a multitude of sins. In the case of the police, it seems to convey a self-righteous attitude that assumes members of the police in-group are the good guys while members of the out-group are potential bad guys. Professionalism enables the police to evade their responsibility of honestly looking at their relationships beyond categories. Perhaps if they were less concerned about becoming professional, they could allow themselves to *be* professional.

---

[2] Jerome H. Skolnick, *Justice Without Trial*, and "The Police Need Help," *Time* (October 4, 1968), pp. 26–27.

The last factor, depersonalization, summarizes my basic criticism of the academy experience. People are defined as things, and the recruits define themselves as cops. Neither side is perceived in terms of complex and ambivalent feelings and thoughts. Discussions, panels, or group therapy sessions are a few of the ways in which recruits might be encouraged to view themselves and others as multifaceted. It seems central, then, that the police academy experience include sessions of self-examination in which recruit and instructor ask themselves why they have become policemen.

There are two major reforms that I believe to be integral to any serious effort to up-grade police training, and by extension, police science programs. One is geared specifically to the training process. It includes the replacement of lectures and technical courses with debates, panels, discussions, and reading assignments that present varied and enlightened viewpoints of major social issues of the day. The second reform focuses on the relationship of the police academy to the total department. I will discuss each of these measures in detail. Of course, there is no perfect solution to police problems, just as there is no perfect solution to any social problem.

PROCESS OF TRAINING

Teaching by means of lectures should be replaced with classes that allow the recruit to express his beliefs and emotional reactions to contemporary social issues, such as student demonstrations and poverty, legal issues such as Supreme Court decisions, and procedural issues such as stopping and frisking. The lecture syle of teaching not only makes learning a passive process but it fails to teach the "whole man." The premise seems to be "we are here to learn [subject], leave your feelings out of it." Yet it is the emotional education of people, not just the intellectual education, which is so desperately needed. In fact, this is one of the facets of education that high school and college students advocate.

The recruit does have to learn a large quantity of information, but the excuse that he has so much to learn in so short a time evades the need to have, emotionally and intellectually, in-depth discussions. Naturally, some subjects lend themselves to lectures better than others; first aid is an example. But the recruit comes to the academy with already formed attitudes that seem similar to his instructors'. The instructors merely articulate his thoughts as, for instance, in the cases of professionalism and Supreme Court rulings. Also facts can be presented rather quickly. For example, instead of a two-hour lecture on the justification of force, the legal prescriptions may be stated along with points that the instructor thinks are important within a half hour to an hour. That leaves a substantial amount of time for a discussion concerning the recruit's *feelings* about using force.

In a previous chapter I divided the academy courses into nine groupings. These included departmental subdivisions and their functions, rules and reports, and patrol procedures. Some of these classes can be streamlined or eliminated. Examples of lectures that can be eliminated without much loss include a full day on arrests led by an FBI agent, fingerprinting, photography, and crime searches. All of these lectures are relevant to detectives, not patrolmen. Special squads serve warrants or take photographs; detectives lead searches of crime scenes and make most of the important arrests. Since it generally takes about five years before a patrolman can become a detective, most of this information, learned during his training, will be forgotten by the time that he can put it to use. If the department believes that some exposure in these areas is necessary, it can be very brief. Why, for instance, is a two-hour lecture on bombs necessary (other than contributing to police solidarity by pointing out the violence in police work)? If a bomb is discovered, the bomb squad is called immediately anyway.

Other subjects that can be shortened include the description of subdivisions such as K-9 and Lost Property, inspections (if neatness is what is really important, not spit-and-polish), and departmental rules and reports. For example, a five-hour lecture on note-taking could be reduced to a couple of hours at the most by allowing the recruit to read the brief handout for 15 minutes or so, instead of reading it to him for a full hour, by giving a further explanation of a few major points, and then leading a question-and-answer period. The many hours devoted to central communications and central records can also be condensed. Not only did the recruit listen to several hours of lectures in both these areas but he also had to spend eight hours over a weekend at these places. One or the other should be eliminated.

In lieu of these mechanical courses, debates and panels should be instituted. If at all possible, group therapy sessions of two or three hours a day for about 10 days should be included, though not used in place of panels, debates, or class discussions. Group therapy is therapy for groups of 10 to 15 persons that are led by trained leaders in order to (1) help remove emotional blocks, (2) develop self-awareness of beliefs and feelings, and (3) develop sensitivity and insight about others and the social environment. If this procedure is too expensive for some departments, the principles of sensitivity and therapy can still be employed in each and every class.

Sensitivity techniques could be helpful to the recruit in gaining an appreciation of the philosophy of the American legal system. Discussions can center on questions such as: Does a law ever become immoral? If so, is there a right to break immoral laws? It is possible or desirable for the law to provide for its own disobedience? Do institutions have primacy over the rights of individuals? If the recruit believes political and legal dissidents are spoiled, immature, misled, or degenerate, they should discuss why they feel that way and should explore the possibility of other interpretations. The strengths and weaknesses of the "truth will out" theory of our legal system should also be explored. In addition, the conflict between public morality and private morality should be debated.

Supreme Court rulings should not be defined as antilaw enforcement by the instructors. Instead, the recruit should discuss why he thinks the decisions impede law enforcement, why the justices decided as they did, and what alternative decisions they could have made. One way to impress the importance of these questions on the recruit is to relate the rulings to his own position vis-à-vis the police department. For instance, during my study some recruits expressed their dissatisfaction over two events. First, a patrolman had been dismissed from the department after he had admitted to the Inspection Squad "off-the-record" that he had broken a major rule. Second, a lecturer informed the recruits that citizen complaints remained in the officer's record even if he were cleared of all charges. In the first case, the recruits believed that the officer should have been warned of his right to remain silent, for he was not, in fact, speaking off-the-record. In the second case, they were disturbed that unfounded complaints would remain in their permanent records.

Likewise, the recruits were angered that the Supreme Court restricted all law enforcers because of certain extreme cases of abuse. It appears that the recruits wanted the very rights that they were willing to deny the citizen. If the recruit is not encouraged to respect the broad legal system and its principles, he will tend to rely on his own sense of justice where there is a conflict of interest.

In-depth discussions may be fitted into police training programs by eliminating some of the classes dealing with specific laws. First, detectives usually take charge of the aftermath of many crimes. Second, some laws can be learned during field work. Finally, laws can be looked up or checked with the desk sergeant if necessary. Laws that should be learned and discussed in depth by the recruit are those that he is most in need of during the course of his work: stop and frisk, justification of force, search and seizure, but especially, peace-keeping laws, such as disorderly conduct. Lessons in these areas could be enhanced by recruits' playing roles of both policemen and offenders.

Panel discussions that include critics of the police should be used throughout police training. Since the major social issues of the day include race relations, military power, women's liberation, education, and police power and the law, panels should be geared toward these subjects. Instead of hearing intended or unintended misinterpretations of various positions by police officers, the recruit can hear and respond to the ideas of minority groups about poverty and the police, students about their ideologies, women about their problems, doctors about marijuana, and lawyers about criminal law. Assigned readings could be used on a regular basis in connection with these panels.

To conclude, there must be a general spirit of inquiry in the police training program that transcends any one particular perspective. Presently, the police seem to be embarked on a course of training that, unfortunately, typifies training programs of other occupations—indoctrination of in-coming members into one school of thought to the exclusion or partial exclusion of competing schools of thought. Of course, in justice to RCPD, it must be recognized that the staff is training unskilled recruits to become competent in the technical aspects of a demanding occupation within an allocated period of only 12 weeks.

Police training should be oriented toward (1) sensitivity to the ambiguities and ambivalences of group and individual interaction, and (2) insight into the recruit's own ideological conflicts and ambivalences. Because the recruit does not have this training, he maintains his rigid stance against unconventional behavior. Based on the response to my discussions with the recruit class, I am convinced that the majority of recruits want to enforce the law fairly and properly. They are not so much prejudiced as they are misinformed about certain current events. Their problem is that they do not actively try to learn on their own other sides of an issue, or they presume that they already know the other sides. The police academy must try to fill this gap. If the recruit is expected to interact with people who have values and expectations different from his own, and if he is not to react intolerantly to certain segments of the population, he must develop the capacity to choose from a collection of responses in order to resolve unexpected or ambiguous situations.[3]

For all practical purposes, I do not think the population from which police candidates are presently selected is going to change. Recruitment policies notwithstanding, the organizational structure of the police must be made more appealing to better prepared candidates whether or not they have a college education. Implementing the recommendations of Skolnick, Wilson, and Manning, which were mentioned at the beginning of this chapter, could be very helpful.

One officer from the New York City Police Department did try to encourage recruitment from Ivy League campuses, but students who applied to various police departments found that one excuse or another was used to reject their candidacy. At any rate, this tack assumes that police reform involves attracting better quality candidates while not recognizing that the system as a whole must be reformed to meet the needs of today. In this spirit, the Task Force Report suggests a plan to increase the representativeness of the members on the police force with the makeup of the patrolled community.[4] It recommends that three levels of requirements, salaries, and responsibilities should be instituted. Consequently, college students, it was predicted, would be attracted to police work, and members of minority groups unable to meet present requirements could enter on more relaxed terms.

Personally, I am skeptical of such a plan. First, a college graduate can still be intolerant and narrowly perceptive, as appears to be the case with many of our "educated" politicians in high offices. Second, I see no reason why minority group members cannot enter on a par with other members of the department. If some offenses can be overlooked (as they fortunately are in RCPD) and requirements relaxed for all candidates, the department can focus on more important issues.

---

[3] Peter Kong-ming New, "The Application of Reference Group Theory to Shifts in Values: The Case of the Osteopathic Students" (unpublished Ph.D. dissertation), University of Missouri, Department of Sociology, 1960, suggests that having many reference groups instead of one, results in insecurity because of conflicting values. A reference group is a group that is used as a point of comparison for evaluating one's self-image or standards of behavior. I take an opposite position. If a person takes a relativistic stance, he can be secure within and tolerant of the conflicting values of multiple reference groups.

[4] President's Commission on Law Enforcement and the Administration of Justice, *Task Force Report: The Police* (Washington, D.C.: Government Printing Office, 1967), Chapter 4.

For instance, a discussion with candidates about social issues can reveal how socially aware or how rigid an individual is. A sensitive patrolman is just as much needed as a formally educated person—probably more so. By sensitive, I mean an openness to recognizing the complexity, ambivalence, and subtlety of feelings, thoughts, and life-styles other than one's own.

STRUCTURE OF TRAINING
The second basic reform involves the commitment of the police department to improve the quality of its training program. This means that more of the resources of the department should be made available to the police academy. These resources include time, money, and personnel. If the recruits are squeezed out of the academy as fast as possible to meet manpower needs, if the academy personnel are not of the very best, and if needed personnel and time for proper training are not forthcoming, patrolmen will be as maltrained as they presently seem to be.[5] Any police administrator who claims that he can improve his training programs without these provisions is dealing only in rhetoric. Unless financial support is provided for lengthy training, for outside speakers (and, perhaps, group therapy leaders), panels, and field trips to places such as mental hospitals, slum areas, and Head Start programs, or for pay incentives for field supervisors, police training will continue to produce defensive and depersonalizing patrolmen. Perhaps, the last remark about pay incentives needs elaboration.

In RCPD the recruit is on probation for 12 months, three of which are spent in the police academy. Theoretically, his training extends into the last nine months but, for all intents and purposes, he is left to his own devices on graduation from the academy. A lack of organizational support for this extended training is revealed when the academy staff continues to hear complaints from precinct commanders who seem to expect the recruit to emerge from the academy competent in all phases of patrol procedures.

Following his academy training, the recruit should receive at least two months of training under the direct supervision of several hand-

---

[5] A Task Force Report Submitted to the National Commission on the Causes and Prevention of Violence, *Politics of Protest*, under the direction of Jerome H. Skolnick (New York: Simon and Schuster, 1969), pp. 255–258.

picked patrolmen. Each supervisory patrolman, because he was selected on his merits and because proper supervision makes more demands on him, should receive a modest remuneration while he acts as supervisor. The role of supervisor is to train the recruit in the patrol procedures that he believes to be the most important. Since the recruit ideally would be supervised by several patrolmen at different times, he would be exposed to different aspects of patrolling. Therefore, while he is with one supervisor for a determined period, he may learn how to handle domestic quarrels. The second supervisor may concentrate on the proper way of handling speeders, while a third may believe it is important for the recruit to learn how to deal with rowdy youths. This two-month period should be followed by the recruit's brief return to the academy (1) to evaluate his field supervision (perhaps, by testing him in the areas covered by his supervisors), (2) to analyze the strengths and weaknesses of his academy training in retrospect, and (3) to explore problems that have emerged from his field work.

The idea of prohibiting patrolmen on probation from carrying firearms should be given some serious consideration. Certainly this can be used on an experimental basis during the two months of directed supervision. The attempt could have two valuable consequences. First, both recruit and patrolman perceive the revolver as integral to police work and to the police image. It would be unthinkable for them to imagine a police officer without a revolver. However, the benefits of carrying a gun while on patrol have never been contrasted and evaluated with the possible greater disadvantages of carrying one. Since most of the patrolman's duties involve keeping the peace rather than enforcing the law, a revolver may not be as necessary as it seems. In fact, carrying a revolver, which can be very intimidating, may interfere with the image of the police officer as friend, counselor, and keeper of the peace.

Second, even if it is found that a revolver is necessary for keeping the peace, the probationer may be encouraged to rely on persuasion through discourse or on his intermediate weapons, such as mace, for controlling people. As was observed in the chapter on defensiveness, the recruits at RCPD saw the revolver not as a last line-of-defense, but as a first line-of-defense. This attitude may change as they become more self-confident, but perhaps they should acquire their confidence before they are issued revolvers.

STRATEGY FOR REFORM

Some claim that police reform requires a more careful selection of police candidates to weed out certain basic personality types. Others suggest that structural considerations should be the prime concern for reform; if the system remains intact, it does not matter what kind of person enters the department—the structure will orient their behavior and attitudes.

Both arguments are correct in part. Surely, it is important to exclude certain kinds of people from police work, such as the sadistic and the intolerant. But if the image of the police is to be changed from one of intolerance and reactionism to one of tolerance and understanding, the members of the department still must be motivated to act in these ways. If the patrolmen are to conform to this new image, *the social structure must provide the opportunities for and give support to attempts to realize this goal.* One's motive to act depends on whether the community usually rewards or punishes such an act. What is regarded as effective or ineffective, moral or immoral, just or unjust is influenced by one's environment. If the police are not motivated to reform themselves in action as well as in word, it may be that the environment (the police organization itself and the community) is perceived as unsupportive of these changes.[6]

Beverly Hills Police Chief Kimball's experience with his Town Board provides one example. By a 3 to 2 vote, the Town Board requested Kimball to resign his position because he did not reflect the desirable image of a Beverly Hills Police Chief. He was charged with attending the 1969 Woodstock, New York youth-rock concert without asking for or receiving the board's permission; talking and joking with a prostitute on a television talk show; and being too tolerant of dissident youth.[7] By its vote, the Town Board was refusing to allow the image of the police to change from one of repression to one of tolerance and understanding. Perhaps the three members of the board were not only voting against Chief Kimball; on an unrecognized and unintended level, they may have been voting to continue having the police do society's dirty work. This meant keeping the police as the "bad

---

[6] Alvin D. Zalinger, "Job Training Programs: Motivational and Structural Dimensions," paper presented at the Research Utilization Conference on Rehabilitation in Poverty Settings, November 1968.

[7] NBC-TV national news, about March 28, 1970. The decision of the Town Board was eventually reversed through the efforts of Beverly Hills youth.

guys" in the eyes of youth by blocking any effective communication between the two groups.

In addition to community support, the patrolman must have organizational support. On a television talk show, police officials in high state and local positions around the nation were asked to discuss their views of youthful political and social dissidents. Predictably, they described youths as being spoiled and immature, and as having no respect for authority or the law. Not one official referred to the social issues that were involved in protests. How can rank-and-file patrolmen be expected to be more open-minded without the support and encouragement of the hierarchy?

Police officials and patrolmen may be quite correct when they claim public stereotypes of law enforcers make attempts at reform too difficult. Nevertheless, if there is to be change, it must start somewhere, and it seems realistic to acknowledge that the burden of proof is on the police, no matter how unfair it appears to be. Thus, the police themselves must initiate change if they want to prevent external agencies from gaining control over some aspects of law enforcement. A further incentive to change might be the implementation of a suggestion made by Senator Robert F. Kennedy. He proposed that the rank-and-file consist of noncareerists who would serve for three years.

It seems that just the willingness of police officers to go out on a limb and experiment along more liberal lines could go a long way toward increasing their stature in the community. If police officials choose to ignore the recommendations of this study, as they seem to have ignored Wilson's, they are only deluding themselves into believing that they will succeed in improving the quality of law enforcement and order maintenance under a system of justice. Custom must *not* reconcile us to everything.

Irrational Idea No. 4: The idea that it is
terrible, horrible, and catastrophic when
things are not going the way one would
like them to go.
Albert Ellis and Robert A. Harper
A Guide to Rational Living

Researcher Role Confusion.

APPENDIX

A serious shortcoming of participant observation studies and methodological texts is the absence of raw data enabling the inquiring student to study the connection between this data and the final written product. The student, who may read very good participatory studies, is often left floundering in his attempt to make sense out of his compilations. While I am unable to go into much detail about how I handled my raw data, those interested will find this information in my doctoral dissertation from which this book stems. Nevertheless, in an attempt to lessen this inadequacy, I offer an uninterrupted and lengthy description of my entry into the field. This description provides a general impression of the pitfalls, responses, and personal adjustments to researcher role definitions by all the parties in the research (researcher, recruits, and academy staff) that necessarily have an influence on the final product. I first discuss the problems of selecting and gaining access to a police academy. This is followed by an account of my first week in the field.

ACADEMY SELECTION AND ACCESS
My first impulse was to seek admittance to the police academy in my home town for four reasons: the department seemed to enjoy a good reputation within the community; I was acquainted with the community, its history, and its unique characteristics; and the community appeared representative of the trend toward highly urbanized suburbs and, therefore, possibly contained a police department representative of those that would exist in the approximate future. Furthermore, it had never been studied before. Other possible departments had been

subject to past research inquiries. Thus, positive or negative attitudes toward these studies may have filtered to academy personnel or recruits. My home town academy was uncontaminated in this sense.

My first appointment with the chief of police took place in November 1966. I was warmly received, and he asked me how soon I could begin the study. After I explained to him that I had yet to complete my Ph.D. course requirements and pass my comprehensive examinations, he gave me tentative permission to enter his academy around September 1968. But because of other academic and financial obligations, I had to postpone my study until early 1969.

I wrote the chief of police requesting an appointment in December 1968 to discuss my proposal and work out its mechanics. He replied that the week during winter recess would be convenient for him. When I arrived at headquarters, however, he sent me to his public relations officer. The latter explained that a study of the department had just been published in which the chief believed his department had been treated unfairly, supposedly because the researchers used poor investigatory methods. (Since all my plans hinged on this one academy, I became sensitized to the obligations that a researcher has to subsequent researchers when he leaves the field.)

The rest of my vacation and the following month were spent writing or calling police departments across the county. Having learned my lesson, I now wanted the security of several academies from which to choose. I spoke with the police commissioner of the very first one I contacted, Rurban County Police Department, and we set up an appointment for early January to discuss the proposal. Only one other department seemed interested, but the refusals of the other departments were revealing of police attitudes toward rsearchers. I interviewed a psychologist who was in charge of training activities in his department. In spite of my explanations of what sociology was and what I hoped to do, he insisted that there would not be enough "excitement" for a sociological study. Another department had been the subject of many research studies, but my participatory strategy was too threatening just then because the department was being investigated by the state and municipality. A third department thought my presence at their academy would make the trainees "uncomfortable." Hence, I had to settle on the first department's overture.

I had an appointment with a chief inspector of Rurban County made through the commissioner. After I arrived, I had serious misgivings about this department, too, since the inspector was away at a meeting in the farthest end of the state. In his place, I saw the commanding officer of the academy, a warm and personable man. He was immediately interested in my proposal and suggested that I assume a cover story: a CIA agent coming for a refresher course, apparently a plausible story there (and which I later found out not to be the case). He seemed impressed, however, with my desire to be completely aboveboard with the recruits rather than to use a cover. He said the next class would begin in the beginning of February; I was to call shortly before then for instructions.

Another department also gave me permission to go through their academy session, which started in March. By now very cautious, I decided to stick with Rurban County in order to have the other to fall back on if circumstances warranted it. This was a fortunate decision, for soon after I began my study at Rurban County, the other department informed me that due to "unforeseen circumstances" (the resignation of the chief of police for a national post) my project would not be possible.

ENTERING THE FIELD

I was instructed to be at headquarters on Monday at 8:00 A.M. When I arrived, I found about 30 men in ties and suits gathered in the hallway entrance. About five men in all stood by themselves; the rest were gathered in groups of three or four. The academy commanding officer and I had agreed that I would tell the recruits that I was a *researcher*. Therefore, I thought it tactful to acquaint a few of the recruits with my identity immediately. I went over to one group, asked if they knew which room we were to report to, got a quick "no," and found no effort to widen the circle to allow me to join the conversation.

I felt rebuffed at this and decided that I should have introduced myself to one of the five loners; but then I spotted an animated—and loosely formed—group. They were discussing the permissiveness of movies and were comparing pay scales of incorporated village police departments within Rurban County. When their interest turned to two young nurses walking by us and up a nearby stairway, I joined in the spirit of the comments and moved into the circle. I tried to say as little as possible, as I thought a participant observer should, making comments only to reaffirm my group "membership." After joking with one of the recruits next to me (John), I asked him if I could look at his orders to report. "Sure, don't you have one?" I replied that I did not because I was a *college student* who had received permission to go through the training course.

Finally, we were directed to a room much like a classroom except for a long table between two flags in the front of the room. I sat in the third row in order to be sure of hearing everything the staff would say. We were instructed by Patrolman Arsenault to remain seated and quiet until the staff arrived, which would be in about an hour. Meanwhile he took roll call. My name was among those men not called, but unlike the rest of them, I did not raise my hand to indicate it. Then he ordered all recruits from Rurban County Department to sit in the front rows and men from the incorporated town departments and other associated agencies to sit in the rear rows. I decided to remain where I was.

The recruit to my right turned to the one sitting directly behind me. They had gone to the same high school and had quit the Megopolis Police Department to join Rurban County. They were comparing their experiences in Megopolis City and making derogatory comments about their job: "I'm glad to be out of that factory," was a theme constantly expressed by other ex-city policemen in the recruit class. As soon as I had established a little rapport by sympathizing with them, I turned to the man next to me and asked if I could see his notice to report. Like John earlier, he inquired if I had one. I answered, "No, I'm a *student writing a Ph.D. paper* on the response of recruits to their training. Nobody seems interested in what the recruits themselves think about it. The police have been dissected and put under the microscope many times; it's time they got more objective and perhaps more sympathetic treatment." He (Paul) agreed and was supportive of the need for such a study to take place.

Suddenly, the name "Harris" boomed out. A sergeant motioned me outside where I was brought to a room across the hall. I was introduced to Lieutenant Noonan, the director of in-service and recruit training, and Captain Anderson, the executive officer, who was second in command at the academy. The sergeant asked me what my purpose was. I replied that I was granted permission to go through the academy and was interested in learning the reaction of the recruits to their training. "Yes, I know, but I just want to get things straight. We'll have to figure out what to do about a gun when we get to that. Have you told anyone who you are?" I answered that I had told several men. He thought it might have been better if I had not told anybody, since it might "scare the recruits." I explained to him I hoped to be aboveboard and not conceal my identity, since the recruits could be helpful if they knew what I was trying to do. The sergeant acknowledged this and said, "Okay, but don't tell anyone else and we'll let the gravevine take its course." Patrolman Arsenault suggested I sit in the back of the room so as not to be conspicuous when the others take the oath during the swearing-in ceremony.

I was left in the room with the captain and lieutenant who tried to pass the time by remarking how "important such a study was," how "it could make a real contribution to the intellectual world," and "it would be good if it could get at things unnoticed by people who were too close to the situation." I gave short answers, not knowing what else to do: should I stand at attention, at parade rest, or at-ease positions? Should I engage in informal conversations with them or behave as I thought someone in a paramilitary organization should? They strained to strike up a conversation, but since I was trying to act like an "actual recruit" with short, abrupt answers to high ranking officers, they were left groping for other topics. One of them related stories of the prejudice of a Southern police department he had recently visited and of the inefficiency of Northeastern departments. This may have been an effort to build up his own department as a consequence of the insecurity of facing a Ph.D. student (very prestigious with the staff) coming to study them.

At last I was permitted to return to the assembly room. I walked by Paul and joked, "I've been sent to the rear of the class." I sat down among the nine or ten incorporated agency recruits. One asked, "What's the matter, did you lose your job?" I smiled and said, "Almost." They asked me if I were from an incorporated village. I explained that I was not; I was *joining Rurban County,* and I was instructed to sit with them until some papers were straightened out. Then my name was called again!

For the second time I was led into the nearby office. This time the police commissioner and the commanding officer of the academy were there. Standing at the military at-ease position as I did previously, they shook my hand, welcomed me, and we all agreed how the study was a great idea, unique, and a breakthrough in police research. And again I felt awkward, not knowing exactly how to react.

It was an awkward situation for all of us. I, for one, had some doubt as to my capacity as a participant observer and the possibility of gleaning anything worthy of a dissertation within a traditionally hostile and secretive occupation. In turn, each staff member told me privately toward the end or after the recruit class graduated from the academy that they were apprehensive over the feasibility of the study, for they were uncertain about the reaction of the recruits toward me. The degree of rapport I was able to establish with the recruits surprised them (and me!) and won their admiration.

When I came back to the room the recruits pressed me for an explanation of what was going on. In desperation I made up the story that my eyesight was still questionable. Thus a foundation was laid for the times whenever I might feel called on to use my glasses. I usually wore glasses, but I kept them in my pocket, since I did not see any other recruit wearing any.

The staff finally came in and were introduced to the class. Following the invocation given by a Rabbi, the commissioner gave a short speech in which he mentioned that 11 men were joining Rurban County Police Department from other law agencies, giving up their seniority and higher pay to do so, and 11 men were members of associated agencies within Rurban County. He congratulated the men on reaching this stage of their careers and then swore in the 42 Rurban County recruits.

The three men nearest the door in the first row were instructed to leave the room. A few minutes later my name was called again, and again I went into the same office. The three recruits were having their pictures taken with the commissioner. After the recruits left, I was brought in for a picture with the commissioner also. While my picture was being taken, the recruit class left headquarters for the academy, which was about five miles away.

Since I had been called from the class three times and was now facing the prospect of arriving at the academy after the others were already there, I was exasperated over the apparent insensitivity that the staff showed with regard to my research position. By calling attention to me, they did not seem to appreciate my delicate position with the recruits, especially since they were the ones who had directed me to assume a disguised role. However, I chalked this up to their ambivalence toward me and my placement within the academy. (More significantly, the staff was not composed of sociological methodologists!)

As I walked into the academy alone, a fellow whom I had noticed staring at me in the hallway at headquarters came up to me and asked, "Don't I know you? Aren't you Richie Harris?" I looked at him and then cried "Bill!" Both of us had been on the same high school track team and ran the same event nine years ago. He asked me what I was doing at the academy, since he had heard I was attending graduate school. In spite of being directed to maintain a disguised identity, I decided to give him a *full explanation*. I was heartened by running into him in this part of the country, for he would be someone to whom I could always turn. Before I could explain that my secrecy was not by choice, we were given the order to fall in. Bill and I stayed together until the class was instructed to rearrange itself by height into three rows. After a brief speech by Patrolman Arsenault, we filed into a classroom. Because I was among the tallest recruits, I found myself in the last row.

Intermittently, requests were called for several recruits at a time to have their uniform measurements taken while Patrolman Arsenault went over the "Rules and Procedures" of the police academy with the remaining recruits. I was the last one to be called. Standing in line, the commanding officer called me over to his office, which was just off the drill floor. I was still anxious about all this attention for "just another recruit." Obviously, I was in some way different from the others. I would have to bluff my way through with excuses in order to reestablish myself with them. The CO gave me the lesson material that the other men were picking up on the drill floor at the same time that they were measured for uniforms: an empty loose-leaf notebook, a hardback notebook, another loose-leaf notebook crammed with the state penal law, traffic law, and code of criminal law, "Rules and Procedures" of the department, and a large manila case bulging with pamphlets and handbooks on traffic identification, first aid, patrol procedures, and police codes. If I felt frustrated about all the attention focused on me, I was equally frustrated with this prospect. How could I possibly learn all that I was handed along with the other recruits and still have time to write out my field notes?

When I went back in line for uniform measurements, I continued my explanation of my *marginal status* which was based on whether or not my vision was acceptable within the standards. Thus I would also have to wait until a shield was issued to me unlike the other recruits, who were receiving them now. But again, I became the unwanted center of attention. When it was my turn to be measured, the CO was called over to check me out, since my name was not on the supplier's roster.

I ate lunch with Bill and explained to him that although I had wanted to be candid with the recruits, the staff thought I could get better results as a disguised participant. He talked about his experiences in the Megopolis Police Department and complained about his training. A recruit sitting nearby, Lucas, joined in the conversation, since he also was from Megopolis City but in its Department of Corrections. He was one of the two recruits who sat next to me in the classroom, and we were to become friendly throughout the training session.

SECOND DAY. By the end of the second day I felt caught up in the excitement of learning something new and making new friends. Participant observers are warned of the possibility of overidentifying with their subjects to the point of injuring research goals by losing their objectivity. Today I felt that danger emerge as I listened to the rousing speeches that made one proud to be a part of the law enforcement institution, as indeed was their purpose. At the same time that I felt myself losing my grasp on an objective perspective, I became aware of my antipathy toward some aspects of police "ideology." It was an ambivalence that lasted throughout the course of the study.

During this day, the recruits heard a lecture on professionalism (part of which is cited in the text) in which law enforcement was pictured as the profession of all the professions. In this lecture, I found themes that were to play important roles in recruit training, for example, professionalism, defensiveness, and solidarity.

Before I went home, I went up to Patrolman Arsenault and requested him to put my name on the roster for roll call; it was awkward for me if one of the recruits noticed my name had not been called. I told some of the recruits that I *would be sworn in* today or tomorrow, so that if my name was placed on the roster, hopefully, everything would fall into place and I could become "one of the guys." By now I felt that my role definition was pretty well contaminated, but starting tomorrow, I thought I could ride it out.

THIRD DAY. I had changed my role from undisguised participant to disguised participant on the first day on the advice of the staff. This role change was followed by a series of unintentional methodological mistakes by the staff in giving me obvious special and individualized attention. On the third day, the impression I had hoped to foster from the first day was seemingly destroyed. It put me in a minor depression for a few days, since I thought my research strategy was ruined. Above all, I had wanted to prevent the following type of incident from occurring, which could have been avoided if I had remained true to myself and to the recruits.

We had just been issued our uniforms, and while the recruits were checking their gear, I was brought to the CO's office. Sergeant Sheehan gave me a shield without a number on it to pin to my cap. He added that the difference in the shield would be noticed by the men eventually. He explained that he really wanted me to be completely disguised, but his orders were not to issue me a bona fide shield. He was also disturbed that so much attention had been drawn to me the first day. After I discussed my research objectives with him again, he was pleased. He asked that I bring anything I felt required immediate change to his attention. I agreed, but immediately realized I would have to renege later if I were to do my study without disturbing the normalcy of the situation.

Then Sergeant Sheehan repeated that it would not be possible for me to maintain a complete disguise among the recruits. I was angry and mortified when I heard this. I silently cursed myself for agreeing with the change in role definition and cursed the staff for not upholding their end of the bargain, which put me in an embarrassing position with the recruits. From the beginning of the whole idea of studying a police academy, I had been sensitive to gaining trust and rapport with a group traditionally hostile to researchers. Confidence in me had to be carefully cultivated. Now I had made excuses, often lying in the process, and I had to revert to my original role definition of *undisguised participant observer*.

After I related the excuses I had made to the recruits to satisfy their curiosity about me, the staff tried to think of a new cover story. Patrolman Arsenault suggested that I tell them I was from the state capitol, and that I was here to learn about police training to *advise the state* on police training and police science curricula. I agreed to this explanation at the time, but later I decided to tell the recruits that I *intended* to be a police adviser and I felt it was important to learn about police work first hand. I eventually added that I was doing the research voluntarily, and soon afterward I admitted that I was also trying to work out a dissertation from the study. This line of reasoning seemed to appeal to the recruits because of the voluntary "roughing it" in police work and appealed to me because it was close to the truth. Bill remained the only recruit aware of the actual circumstances.

Rather than mix with the recruits after leaving the office, I headed straight toward Bill, in whom I could confide. Lucas was with him: "Hey, what's going on in there; are you sworn in yet?" I replied that I had just been given permission to admit that I was going through the academy in a *civilian capacity*. Lucas responded, "I knew something was going on; usually I'm the one who gets stuck without a uniform and things go wrong with." I put as much blame as I could on the staff for the deception. I explained, "I wanted the men to know what I was doing here from the very beginning, but the staff ordered me not to tell them. Now they say, tell them. I feel so embarrassed after making all those excuses before." Lucas sympathized, "Yeah, yeah, I know how it is."

As recruits curiously came up to me and asked what was happening, I became satisfied that generally they did not feel that I tried to "put one over on them" when I offered my new cover story. Apparently, obeying orders, even for clandestine activities, was not something to feel resentful about. Perhaps the crisis was only in my own guilt.

FOURTH DAY. On the fourth day all of us were required to come in full uniform. I arrived a little concerned about my equipment because

I did not know in what order to position my whistle, handcuff case, bullet case, or holster on my belt. Bill quickly spotted the misarrangement and told me the proper order. Then I went to the office to pick up my shield for my shirt, but the staff was unable to locate it just then. Insecure because the missing shield made me stand out and still mortified over my previous deception, I stayed with Bill and Lucas until we were to fall in for inspection.

I felt relaxed during the long inspection. But when Sergeant Sheehan reached me, he asked, "Your uniform is not pressed, why isn't it pressed?" Since the uniform was new and neatly folded, I never thought about the need to iron it. I answered, "No excuse, sir," as I thought a military answer should be. "Do you have a better pair of shoes?" "Yes, sir." My black shoes which I had intended to spit-shine were still at the shoe repair store because I had not been able to pick them up on time. The sergeant seemed determined not to go on to the next recruit: "Trousers have to be shortened quite a bit." Finally, he passed on to the next man, and I began to stop sweating—until the inspection team went down the back of the row and Patrolman Arsenault whispered, "Suck in that gut!"

An announcement was made that the first hour of classes would be for county recruits alone. Associated agency recruits were given an extended coffee break. Although it was the first and only time I felt like a snoop, an outsider listening to privy information, the lecture was an eye-opener for me. The lecturer was the president of the Police Brotherhood Association, the police union. He was urging the recruits to join the PBA because of the benefits that the union had already won or was fighting for, such as higher salaries, full pay for rookies even while they were going through their training, free medical, dental, and life insurance plans, a dollar a day annuity, and more vacation time with pay. He also explained the politicking involved in winning these demands. When some of the recruits complained that the minimum pay should be higher, I became silently resentful. Their pay during training, $7500 per year, was more than the $6000 I earned for teaching full-time with an M.A. degree and much higher than the $2800 I averaged for two and one-half years as a teaching assistant in graduate school while earning my Ph.D. Thus, there are not only strategy problems of properly defining and communicating one's research role, but also problems of distorting data out of hostility and resentment.

During lunch, Arthur, one of the recruits to whom I attached myself because of his witty insights, walked up to me: "Hey, are they really not giving you a gun with a firing pin?" I could not remember if I had mentioned that to him yesterday or if he had just heard it through the

grapevine. I said, "That's right." He seemed surprised and amused:
"Oh, that's ridiculous. What do they expect you to do? 'Okay, you
guys, come on out or I'll spit on you!' " He and the nearby recruits
criticized the staff so much, I felt obliged to defend them. "Now wait a
minute. Rurban County is really taking a chance with me; they're
sticking their necks out—I could be writing an exposé." Arthur then
asked, "Tell me, what are you doing?" Another recruit answered
before I could finish taking a breath to reply. "He's auditing the course.
He's taking it for his own benefit so he can go back to college and
tell his students about police work." Arthur mocked, "Okay, class,
now when you see a cop reach over to the left side of his pocket,
watch out." I broke in and added that I also wanted to know about
actual police work before I attempted to advise anyone about academy
training or police science courses.

Suddenly the conversation turned to the benefits for which the PBA
was fighting: "That'll be a good deal if all those things of the PBA go
through." I left the table soon after this point. As I mentioned, I felt
a bit resentful of that topic at the moment. On the one hand, I thought
I should force myself to listen, but I provided myself with the convenient excuse that I must really write down the other conversations
at the lunch table before formation. I always used the last few minutes
of lunch hour to jot down key items of lunch conversations in the
protection of the latrine.

At the coffee break, before our last class of the day, I pulled aside
Danny, the other recruit who sat beside me. I wanted to tell him personally about my new "identity" before he heard it second hand. I
explained how the staff changed their minds about my not telling
anyone about my civilian status, and then I gave him my new cover
story as someone interested in police advisory work. Danny replied,
"I thought there was something; you seemed to be writing so much.
So that's why you were called out the first day." He said he did not
mind the subterfuge: he was merely wondering why I was writing so
much, even when the lecturers did not seem to be saying anything
significant.

Two other recruits walked up to us while I was explaining my status,
and they asked what we were talking about. I repeated that I was
trying to learn about academy training in order to advise police
administrators about their training programs, and I believed a higher
level of understanding was attained by experiencing what the recruits
had to go through. I added that I was granted the power of privileged
information in case they were distrustful of me. One of them remarked,
"Oh, you're the one." I asked him what he meant. "I saw someone

with all the brass not at attention on the first day." I said that I was still at an at-ease position with them. "Yeah, but nobody does that with those guys." They agreed that my idea was good and seemed to respect me for volunteering to go through the training myself. Later that day when I apologized for being less than candid with a recruit, he simply shrugged, "Well it's your business anyway."

After the last class, physical training, some of the recruits staggered into the latrine where most of us were changing from our sweat clothes back into our uniforms. One of them gasped to me, "This stuff is tough, and you're doing it on your own." I said sarcastically, "I hope you guys appreciate it now," and we laughed.

FIFTH DAY. On this last day of the week, I finally got my county shield. It was the same as the recruits' shields except my numbers were S191 instead of the four numbers that would be consecutive to theirs. All the recruits of Rurban County had consecutive numbers to each other depending on who had scored higher on the Civil Service examinations; the next class would begin with the number after the last number where our class left off.

I was excited about finally receiving my shield and proudly showed it off to the other recruits. This induced more recruits to be more direct in their curiosity about me, and again I had to explain my purpose at the academy. This time I finally added that I was *hoping to get a dissertation* out of my experiences. After I had explained who I was and what I was trying to do (which by now was very close to the truth) to one group, it seemed another group or individual would ask me the same question. Clearly the recruits must have been entirely confused about my identity during the week, and this situation was not helped by my many different explanations.

As I was putting my cap and shield into my locker at the end of the day, Sergeant Sheehan asked me if I would hand in a critique of the training program each of the three times that the other recruits would do so. I said I would be pleased to, but that if I did write the critiques before the end of the training session, they might influence the staff or lecturers to revamp part of their program. In effect, that would destroy the validity of my study, since I would be contributing to a change in academy training while my research was still in progress. To my relief, he understood my position in spite of his obvious concern for some kind of feedback.

*   *   *   *   *

From my description of my first week at the academy, the obvious question arises. How did these experiences and problems affect the outcome of the study? As Blanche Geer realized, the first few days in the field do have an impact on the perspective of the researcher and the data that he decides to collect.[1] In my case, for example, my own attitudes and behavior throughout the course of the study may have been influenced to a certain extent by the events of the third day. Feeling mortified over the need to change from disguised to undisguised participant, I stuck with the recruits with whom I felt most comfortable for the rest of that day. Could I have found more valuable information if I had forced myself to join other groups?

Perhaps researcher bias did influence the description and evaluation of the three basic themes. That is, a case could be made that these themes were my own projections. There is evidence that a study may reveal more about the researcher involved than it does about his subjects.[2] My notes of the first week certainly indicate my feelings of defensiveness vis-à-vis the recruits and staff. How much of the defensiveness that I "saw" stemmed from my own defensiveness? Also, until I was later enlightened by a women's lib friend, I could have been projecting my own concept of masculinity in my interpretation of the man-of-action image that seemed to prevail. Finally, how much depersonalization was a reflection of my own self-image as a researcher who had to be detached and was, therefore, dehumanized?

The existence of a connection between my philosophies and the data that I collected cannot be denied. The problem, however, is to determine in what ways and to what extent the data were distorted by my projections. It may be impossible for me to answer this question objectively. For that reason, it behooves other researchers to study police training in order to compare and contrast my results with their own. Until there are comparative studies of police training, we shall not know to what degree my conclusions were based on erroneous assumptions and distorted data.

---

[1] Blanche Geer, "First Days in the Field," *Sociologists at Work*, edited by Phillip E. Hammond (Garden City, N.Y.: Doubleday, 1967), pp. 372–398.
[2] Loren J. and Jean Chapman, *Psychology Today*, 5 (November 1971), pp. 18–22ff; Kai Erikson, "A Comment on Disguised Observation in Sociology," *Social Problems*, 14 (Spring 1967), pp. 366–373; and Neil Friedman, *The Social Nature of Psychological Experiments* (New York: Basic Books, 1967).

Index